A Feminist Manifesto for Education

A Feminist Manifesto for Education

Miriam E. David

polity

First published in 2016 by Polity Press

Polity Press
65 Bridge Street
Cambridge CB2 1UR, UK

Polity Press
350 Main Street
Malden, MA 02148, USA

ISBN-13: 978-1-5095-0426-8
ISBN-13: 978-1-5095-0427-5(pb)

A catalogue record for this book is available from the British Library.

Library of Congress Cataloging-in-Publication Data

Names: David, Miriam E.
Title: A feminist manifesto for education / Miriam E. David.
Description: Cambridge, UK ; Malden, MA : Polity Press, 2016. | Includes
  bibliographical references and index.
Identifiers: LCCN 2016000779| ISBN 9781509504268 (hardback) | ISBN
  9781509504275 (pbk.)
Subjects: LCSH: Feminism and education. | Women--Education. | Sexism in
  education.
Classification: LCC LC197 .D37 2016 | DDC 371.822--dc23 LC record available at http://
lccn.loc.gov/2016000779

Typeset in 11 on 13 pt Monotype Bembo by
Servis Filmsetting Ltd, Stockport, Cheshire
Printed and bound in Great Britain by CPI Group (UK) Ltd, Croydon

For further information on Polity, visit our website: politybooks.com

Contents

Acknowledgements

This book is based upon a great deal of collaborative and collective research, over many years, and I am very grateful to all the people that I have shared with. In particular, I would like to thank the women who participated in my international study of feminist academics and educators, without whose conversations and ideas this book would not have been possible. I am also very grateful to my colleagues on the European Union's Daphne-III Programme, 'GAP Work: Improving gender-related violence intervention and referral through youth practitioner training' (JUST/2012/DAP/AG/3176) (2013–2015): especially, the coordinator Dr Pam Alldred of Brunel University, London, and Dr Barbara Biglia, Universitat Rovira i Virgili, Tarragona, Spain, who contributed to chapters 2, 3 and 5 and without whom I could not have completed the book. Their collegiality and friendship are legendary. Jonathan Skerrett of Polity Press has also been immensely supportive and helpful.

I should also like to thank my family, particularly my children – Dr J. Toby Reiner and his partner Dr Margaret Winchester; and Ms Charlotte Reiner Hershman and her husband David Hershman – and my partner, Professor Jeffrey G. Duckett.

The book is dedicated to my grandson – Jacob Hershman – and all children and young people of future generations, in the hope that they may have more respectful and fair lives than is possible at present.

Abbreviations

ACJ	Catalan Youth Agency, Catalonia, Spain
ACU	Association of Commonwealth Universities
AERA	American Educational Research Association
AIDS	Auto-Immune Deficiency Syndrome
AHEAD	Against Homophobia: European Local Administration Devices
AHRC	Arts and Humanities Research Council, UK
ASA	American Sociological Association
ASHE	Association for the Study of Higher Education
AYP	About Young People, a British community and youth organization.
BERA	British Educational Research Association
BJSE	*British Journal of Sociology of Education*
BME	Black and Minority Ethnic groups
BSA	British Sociological Association
BWSG	Bristol Women's Studies Group
CAMFED	Campaign for Female Education
CEDAW	Convention on the Elimination of All Forms of Discrimination Against Women
CND	Campaign for Nuclear Disarmament
CR	Consciousness-raising groups
CREG	Centre for Research on Education and Gender
CYP	children and young people
DE	Department of Education of the Catalonia Government, Spain

DEVAW	Declaration on the Elimination of Violence Against Women
DV	domestic violence
EC	European Commission
ECU	Equality Challenge Unit, for UK HE
EEC	European Economic Community
EEO	equal [educational] opportunities
EFA	Education For All
EHRC	Equalities and Human Rights Commission, UK
EIGE	European Institute for Gender Equality
ERA	European Research Area
ESF	European Science Foundation
ESRC	Economic and Social Research Council, UK
EU	European Union
EVAW	End Violence Against Women coalition, UK
FDR	Franklin Delano Roosevelt, US President from 1933 to 1945
FE	further education
FGM	female genital mutilation
FWSA	Feminist and Women's Studies Association
GAP	GAP Work: Improving gender-related violence intervention and referral through youth practitioner training' (JUST/2012/DAP/AG/3176) (2013–2015) (European Union's Daphne-III Programme)
GBV	gender-based violence
GDP	gross domestic product
GEA	Gender and Education Association
GEXcel	Gender and Equality Centre of Excellence
GPI	Gender Parity Index
GRV	gender-related violence
HE	higher education
HESA	Higher Education Statistical Agency
HIV	human immunodeficiency virus
IMF	International Monetary Fund
INSTRAW	International Research and Training Institute for the Advancement of Women
IOE	Institute of Education, University College London

IWD	International Women's Day, celebrated on 8 March for over 100 years
IWI	International Women's Initiative
LGBTQi	lesbian, gay, bisexual, transgender, queer, intersexual
LMU	London Metropolitan University
LSE	London School of Economics and Political Science
MDG	Millennium Development Goal
MOD	Ministry of Defence, UK
MP	Member of Parliament, UK
MRC	Medical Research Council
MS	The early US feminist magazine founded by Gloria Steinem
NAC	National Abortion Campaign
NAWO	National Association of Women's Organizations
NCCL	National Council of Civil Liberties, UK
NGO	non-governmental organization
NOW	National Organization of Women, USA
NUSEC	National Union of Societies for Women's Citizenship, UK
NUWSS	National Union of Women's Suffrage Societies, UK
OECD	Organization for Economic Cooperation and Development
OISE	Ontario Institute for Studies in Education, University of Toronto, Canada
OU	Open University, UK
PG	postgraduate students
PhD	Doctor of Philosophy
PGCE	Postgraduate Certificate of Education
PgDip HE	Postgraduate Diploma in Higher Education
PM	Prime Minister
PSA	public service announcements, USA
PSED	public sector equality duties, UK
PSHE	personal, social and health education
ROW	Rights of Women, a British feminist legal organization.

SPA	Social Policy Association, UK
SRE	sex or sexualities and relationships education
SRHE	Society for Research in HE
STEM	science, technology, engineering and maths and/or medicine subjects
TU	trade union
UCAS	University and College Agency for Students, UK
UCU	Universities and Colleges Union, UK
UG	undergraduate students
UK	United Kingdom of Great Britain and Northern Ireland
UN	United Nations
UNESCO	United Nations Educational, Scientific and Cultural Organization
UNIFEM	United Nations Development Fund for Women (no longer exists)
URV	University Roviri i Virgili, Catalonia, Spain
USA	United States of America
UUK	Universities UK, the organization of UK leaders of HE
VAW[G]	violence against women [and girls]
VSO	Voluntary Service Overseas
WACC	Women's Abortion Campaign
WE	Women's Equality Party, UK
WEA	Workers' Educational Association
WHEM	Women in HE Management
WHO	World Health Organization
WL	Women's Liberation/Lib
WLM/WM	Women's Liberation Movement or Women's Movement
WNC	Women's National Commission, UK
WOW	Women of the World
WS	Women's Studies courses
WSPU	Women's Social and Political Union, UK
WSWW	Women's Studies Without Walls
WTC	Women's Therapy Centre

Introduction

This book is a feminist manifesto for education. First, I present what is now known about gender and sexual relations through feminist, educational and social research, given the increasingly widespread international public debates about sexual abuse, bullying, harassment and overarching violence against women and girls (VAWG). Second, I draw from this voluminous research and policy-based evidence a series of pointers as to how we could develop a fairer, more equal and gender-conscious education for both boys and girls, including those with diverse sexualities and from ethnic, racialized, classed families. This 'manifesto' would ensure a society that is more socially just, safe and free from violence for both men and women.

In particular, I draw on a specific European Union (EU)-funded project about how to challenge gender-related violence (GRV) amongst children and young people by working with educators and trainers (Alldred and David 2015; Alldred and Biglia 2015). This is a feminist activist project in which I have been involved with British, Irish, Italian and Spanish colleagues and others across Europe, over the last two years. The EU's Daphne programmes commenced at the beginning of the twenty-first century, as a result of international feminist and women's campaigning about women and children's rights over the previous quarter-century. The Daphne programmes consist of action and education or training projects to transform gender and sexual relations. They are also linked to developing the research base on how to improve knowledge and understanding about such relations. This research has been developed by second and subsequent waves of feminists, particularly in academia, although working with community and local activists.

Given this and other feminist, educational and social research with which I have been involved (David 2003, 2014), I identify what could be done to transform relations between boys and girls, and men and women, given the rise of sexualization within new media, through both policy and practice. I bring together several diverse fields of endeavour: feminist work on gender, sexualities, women and education, on gender or sexual violence, on children and families, and policy critiques, especially around neoliberalism and individualization.

These different fields are not usually brought together even amongst feminists, of whatever wave or tendency, and are often heavily contested. This book is not simply a dispassionate approach, but a plea for better and more critical forms of education and schooling to make gender and sexual relations central to forms of schooling for children and young people. It is based upon a passionate commitment to sexual, social and gender equality; respect and fairness; freedom from violence; hence the notion of manifesto.

Inevitably, the book goes beyond traditional political manifestos that are usually statements of values and intent about policy change within a narrow time frame and linked with political expediency. I want to tease out how the aims of social, civil and human rights movements for change, including feminism and the women's liberation movement (WLM), might be more effectively embedded in progressive and social forms of education and schooling to enable such socio-political transformations.

I will explore the evidence on which to base such change, in particular looking at what feminist educators and social scientists have revealed over the last fifty years about gender and sexual relations, and about the critical importance of forms of feminist, progressive or radical education. This also means going beyond the traditional debates about equal opportunities, including social and gender equalities, to understand how gender and sexuality are deeply embedded in cultural, ethnic and social relations. It also entails considering the resistances, both psychological and political, to changing power relations, whether about patriarchy, male domination, sexism or misogyny. These are all contested fields of feminist, educational and social research, around changing concepts of gender and sexuality, especially lesbian, gay, bisexual, transsexual, queer or intersexual (LGBTQi).

Clearly, there are complex arguments about how important education is to social change. It has been seen as vital to aid the processes of socio-cultural change and yet it is clear that education is also a tool to reproduce the status quo, or traditional social class and family relations: that it does not alter social hierarchies and political elites. Indeed, at this particular political juncture, it does appear that there is great resistance to such change. Over the last fifty years, there have been contested arguments about both the form and content of social change, not only in the UK, but across Europe and North America, the so-called global North, and linked with former colonies too.

The Transforming Global Socio-Economic and Political Contexts

There has been a major shift from the British postwar political consensus around social democracy and the welfare state, to a renewed and revised form of individualism and limited forms of state intervention in ensuring social and individual welfare for men and women in the twenty-first century. This move towards neoliberalism began in the 1980s under, ironically, the first female Prime Minister, the Conservative Margaret Thatcher. She joined forces with the then Republican President of the US, Ronald Reagan, and an inexorable process of globalization and neoliberalism was set in train.

Over the last thirty years or so, there have been international shifts towards globalization, clearly linked with forms of global capitalism and the role of education as a central and critical component. This is now known as 'academic capitalism' (a term coined by the American feminist Sheila Slaughter in 1997) or the 'knowledge economy'. This is also the case in other countries of Europe, most of which are now linked together through the EU. The forms of social welfare and social protectionism for men and women have shifted unevenly as various countries have joined the EU (such as the UK, Ireland and Spain). And countries of the British Commonwealth, such as Australia, Canada and New Zealand, have also developed in this fashion.

Similarly, the language and discourses about gender and sexual equality and relations have changed, as have the campaigning and political contexts incorporated, to some extent, in changing socio-economic systems. It is only during the last fifty years that the notion of gender as a social construction has entered social, legal and political discourse, in part as a result of feminist activism and associated social movements around forms of sexuality and transsexual or transgender relations. Gender equality as a concept is now accepted as integral to the political and legal discourse of neoliberalism, although its radical and transformative potential has become muted through its incorporation into such discourses. Gender equality as a matter of numbers or proportions now stands in marked contrast to some radical forms of feminist activism under neoliberal regimes.

Yet both gender equality and liberal feminism have been incorporated into these new discourses, evacuating all progressive meaning from them. And though 'feminism' is a term on the public and media agenda today, which it was not even as recently as at the turn of the twenty-first century, its meanings have changed with the advent of neoliberalism, as the American feminist-socialist Nancy Fraser (2013) argues, claiming that feminism is now the handmaiden of capitalism.

In 2015, in the UK, for example, patriarchal or sexist politics hold sway, although there are some paradoxical processes at work: there are more women in Parliament, making up a third of elected members, but they remain in relatively subordinate positions. Similarly, there are also more explicitly gay and lesbian Members of Parliament (MPs) (thirty-two in fact). Moreover, Conservative Prime Minister David Cameron, re-elected in May 2015, has appointed more women to his Cabinet than there have been in any British Cabinet before: women number over 40 per cent. How many of these women are committed to feminism, gender equality and social transformation? This is a paradox of socio-political change under neoliberalism. These changes in gender balance are occurring in many countries of the global North, most recently in the case of Canada, with the election of the Liberal, Justin Trudeau, who declared himself a feminist and appointed a Cabinet of fifty per cent women, in October 2015. On the other hand, the socialist female Prime Minister of Australia, Julia Gillard, was ousted in 2013 in a campaign that she described in the Australian Parliament as misogynistic.

Despite the Europe-wide context of a commitment to neo-liberal gender equality, gender politics barely enters the fray in the UK, with the battle lines drawn around the same old family values, assigning power to men, and subordinate status to women. Curiously, arguments still rage about the role of political leaders' wives, albeit that they are no longer confined to the kitchen. There are relatively rare debates about women as leaders in their own right, and sardonic comments about the fact that the leaders of the Green Party, the Scottish National Party and Plaid Cymru, for example, are 'self-proclaimed feminists'.

The announcement that Hillary Clinton would run for the Democratic Party nomination for US President mentioned that she too is a 'self-proclaimed feminist'. Clinton is seen as a 'second-wave feminist to the bone', meaning that she has liberal feminist sentiments (Freeman 2015). Gloria Steinem (2015), a founder of *Ms.* magazine, as a second-wave feminist is supportive of Clinton and also other American public figures such as Sheryl Sandberg. Sandberg is the Chief Operating Officer of Facebook. Her *Lean In*, published in 2013, has been seen as a new feminist manifesto or 'Betty Friedan for the digital age' (Dowd 2013). This kind of 'liberal feminism' is at odds with other radical political stances, which focus more on social inclusion, but it can incorporate gender equality and a liberal stance on dealing with VAWG. These tensions between forms of feminism in relation to gender equality and GRV are to be explored.

While abuse and VAWG appear to be on the rise, as they are frequently on the public agenda, I argue that this represents a relatively new public identification of a previously hidden social issue. Over the last half-century, radical feminism, as Mackay (2015: 13) argues, has been critically important to raising this secret into a public question, yet it remains an unresolved political dilemma. Indeed, in some places, cultures or religions, the traditional sexual and gender relations of certain nations and countries, including violence and harassment, are justified and even sanctified, and women's cultural, economic, legal and social independence abhorred.

There has been some welcome change in the balance of political arguments, and there has been some movement towards feminism in public places and spaces with the resurgence of popular feminism in the twenty-first century. Indeed, the idea of manifestos has also been extended to a wider discussion of political values, including about women. For example, the British Labour Party published a *Manifesto for Women*, pulling out of their general manifesto for the General Election in May 2015 the key elements that affected women.

They emphasized: '6 things you need to know about Labour's plan for women and equality'. These were about low pay, and women as 'parents', with their young children and in families and public life. Most importantly, the manifesto stated that:

> Violence against women and girls is never acceptable, so Labour will put tackling it at the heart of government. We will appoint a new commissioner to enforce national standards on tackling domestic and sexual abuse, strengthen the law and provide more stable central funding for women's refuges and Rape Crisis Centres. And we'll work to prevent violence, introducing age appropriate compulsory sex and relationship education in schools. (UK Labour Party 2015: 3)

This Labour manifesto for women was different from traditional approaches, but it is clear that it was too radical for UK sensibilities during the 2015 General Election. The Fawcett Society showed how very limited other parties were in their overall approaches to women and gender equality, and how limited the approach to VAWG was. Only the Labour Party hinted at using schooling as a means of prevention, basing this on recent feminist and social research. Although the Labour Party was defeated at the General Election, and this manifesto has disappeared, it marks an important step in the development of a renewed political consciousness about women, gender and education.

On the other hand, as a result of wider international feminist campaigning, including for dealing with VAWG, such as the creation of the celebratory annual Women of the World (WOW) events linked to the international 'A Million Women Rise' (founded by the redoubtable American playwright Eve Ensler) and International Women's Day (IWD), in the last decade a new British political party has been spawned. This is the Women's Equality (WE) Party, founded by feminist broadcaster Sandi Toksvig. This political party was launched at WOW in March 2015 and has been gathering political momentum through social media. The manifesto of this party also includes statements about both education and violence against women. It states that:

> it's time for a new voice in British politics – a non-partisan force determined to put equality for women at the top of the national agenda . . . we have determined the core issues: equal representation in politics and the boardroom, equal pay, equal parenting rights, equality of and through education, equal treatment by and in the media and an end to violence against women.

WE's mission statement continues:

> Equality for women isn't a women's issue. When women fulfil their potential, everyone benefits. Equality means better politics, a more vibrant economy, a workforce that draws on the talents of the whole population and a society at ease with itself . . . bringing together

women and men of all ages and backgrounds, united in the campaign
for women to enjoy the same rights and opportunities as men so that
both sexes can flourish.

These are illustrations of the ways that women's issues, women's
equality and education, and, separately, VAWG are now on the
political agenda, albeit controversially. The Labour Party buries
its commitments, while the WE Party reverts to very traditional
sexual politics and gender binaries. So precisely what are the ways
forward for women's or gender equality that also attend to issues
about VAWG? How do we facilitate change, linking with other
issues to do with children and young people? What have we learnt
from international feminist educational and social research? What
in particular have second-wave feminists, who entered higher education (HE) as it began to expand to fit the needs of the economy,
contributed to these debates and how can we use their insights for
the future?

I will build upon issues specifically concerning how to teach
about girls' and women's positions in the wider world. These
entail looking historically at the changing roles of women in politics, through transformations in women's suffrage, perceiving the
extent of the struggle for emancipation by nineteenth- and twen-
tieth-century women, often dubbed 'first-wave feminists', which
amounted to a very violent fight. This included police brutality,
imprisonment and force-feeding in the UK, with similar events in
other countries, especially the long-drawn-out struggles in the US,
culminating in the Nineteenth Amendment in 1920.

Developing philosophical and political arguments about equality of respect and lack of discrimination is also vital to this
endeavour. For example, the consideration about LGBTQi has
rarely been focused upon and, where it is, it is usually about
gay men. This is yet another dilemma to consider in looking at
developing a fairer, more equal and respectful education. In terms
also of the literature on LGBTQi, there is less about lesbianism,
which is a heavily silenced topic, than gay men. For example,
in a recently published philosophic tract about such discrimination, Paul Bailey (2007) looked at the silencing and oppression

of homosexuality around the world. He focused on cultural and religious repression, leading to violence against male homosexuals, for the most part sidelining lesbianism or being 'post-heterosexual' (Orbach and Winterson 2015).

In a series of books about *Manifestos for the 21st Century*, the second-wave socialist feminist Beatrix Campbell (2013) wrote *End of Equality*, subtitled *The Only Way is Women's Liberation*. This is a sustained argument for the necessity of socially inclusive feminism, on which I wish to build, to ensure a more socially and sexually just world by transforming economic and social relations. Campbell's is a careful dissection of the socio-economic trans-formations under neoliberalism, to develop new approaches. She ends with the rallying cry: 'to paraphrase from the Manifesto of the Communist Party once more: Feminism is already acknowledged by all its powers to be itself a power; it is high time that feminism meets this myth of the "Spectre of Feminism" with its own new manifestos' (2013: 92).

Manifestos for the Twenty-first Century

Thus, my manifesto will build upon a complex array of inter-national strategies about gender equality in education, linked to issues specifically around dealing with VAWG, as well as detailed feminist academic and activist evidence. Campbell's manifesto, excellent though its argument is, is not at all about young women or schooling and ways to learn to transform sexual relations. Her argument is entirely about how feminist arguments for women's liberation and sexual equality have become subsumed within a neoliberal economic system and no longer provide for genuine gender equality.

But Campbell argues that we are now in a new conjuncture of a

neopatriarchal and neoliberal matrix that assails – and provokes – feminism's renaissance. This is the new form of articulation of men's dominance over women – from sexual violence to human rights

protocols and equality laws, budgets, time, money and care. A new
sexual settlement is being made. But it is unsustainable . . . Imagine
men without violence. Imagine sex without violence . . . it is doable,
reasonable and revolutionary. (2013: 91–2)

A précis of her book is also included in an edited collection (Hall,
Massey and Rustin 2015). This is a critique seeking 'to map the
political, economic, social and cultural contours of neoliberalism
. . . and call into question the neoliberal order itself, and find
radical alternatives to its foundational assumptions.' Massey and
Rustin argue: 'In 2013 we – along with our fellow founding editor
of *Soundings*, Stuart Hall – decided to . . . bring together . . . an
online Manifesto. The idea was to form an analysis of the political
context that was both unifying and systemic, but was also respectful to the particularities of the issues and areas of society to be
discussed' (2015: 7–8).

Campbell (2015) focuses on how neoliberalism, forms of state
and civil society and rampant capitalism are a breeding ground for
violence and gender polarization. She focuses on gender rather
than WLM, arguing that:

Violence is not unthinking, visceral, primitive: it is produced by, and
is productive of, power over land, riches and people. Violent hyper-
masculinities and concomitant gender polarization are, therefore,
not residual: they are remade in civil society and in state apparatuses.
Indeed the violence that neoliberal capital and its accomplices generate
is an integral part of its evolving gender settlement – which I call neo-
patriarchy. (2015: 69–85)

Her argument is very similar to Fraser's (2013) and mine: about
the incorporation of gender into new forms of capitalism and
associated neoliberal politics. She goes on to state:

in spite of this increased violence, and the inequality that is inherent
in neoliberalism, in the last quarter of a century the world's institutions reached a consensus: *they joined together in hailing the goal of
gender equality*. Ironically, this was at the very moment when we were

witnessing the limits, the exhaustion, of the equality paradigm. The notion of equal opportunity was, in any case, incapable of withstanding the structures of gender: the sexual division of labour, and violence as a resource in the making and doing of masculinity . . . collapse of postwar consensus on welfare states and the mixed economy . . . They preach equal opportunity, but in practice produce 'regressive modernization'. (2015: 71; my emphasis)

Expanding her definition of the neoliberal and neo-patriarchal matrix, she states that 'Global capitalism works with patriarchal principles, institutions, cultures and psyches. So our liberation from this tragedy is inconceivable – it is, literally, unthinkable – without feminism' (ibid.: 72). Her conclusion remains that of her manifesto book: to argue for a radical and socialist feminist transformation. This is exactly what I also want to do, using education, and schooling especially, as the means.

Manifestos for Education

'One of the most profound ways in which we show our respect for other people is by treating them as capable of engaging in reasoned argument and discrimination: in other words, as equals in intellect and humanity' (Collini 2010). Quite clearly, this is vitally important to any form of education. Within the professional education community, two new contrasting manifestos for education have also recently been published, which emphasize respect and equality.

First of all, COMPASS (2015), an independent think-tank emerging from the British Labour Party in the early twenty-first century, has worked on developing a strong argument about the future of schooling and education. They entitled their publication *Big Education: Learning for the 21st Century*. The argument is about how to reframe education, schooling and teaching in relation to changing forms of the political economy in the twenty-first century. Yet the report remains gender-blind and not at all attentive to issues about gender equality or dealing with VAWG, unlike the Labour *Manifesto for Women*.

Second, and by contrast, the British Educational Research Association (BERA) has produced 'an evidence-based policy manifesto that respects children and young people', entitled *Fair and Equal Education* (2015). This manifesto illustrates how to integrate feminist and educational research, although the term 'feminist' is not used. In the foreword, it was argued that an array of educational research was provided to appeal to policymakers:

> This Manifesto emerges from . . . review[ing] a wide range of research . . . with a view to drawing together the implications for policy . . . As we approach[ed] the UK General Election in May 2015, [we] . . . prepared a Manifesto setting out an agenda for a fair and equal education that has the interests of children and young people at its heart. (2015: 1)

The central argument is that

> Children and young people are entitled to an education that . . . develops their personality, talents and abilities to the full. Fair and equal education recognises differences in children and young people's experiences, interests and backgrounds and ensures equality in access and provision. Over the last 40 years, evidence from educational research has told us about the extent of inequality. It has also told us how to make education more equal and fair . . . By addressing these key areas we can achieve the kind of education needed to respect children and young people's entitlement to quality education. We recognise that the path to achieve such gains requires a long-term vision, including further research. However, to protect and promote children and young people's educational entitlements, the UK Government can take . . . immediate steps towards achieving the goal of fair and equal education. (2015: 2–3)

While the authors do not address feminist educational research explicitly, what is most attractive and interesting about their arguments is how gender, sexuality and sexual health issues are threaded throughout. They conclude the manifesto by asserting recommendations:

> Looking to the future . . . together we need to . . . reframe our understandings of 21st century Britain that are more reflective of our globalised world. We need to promote inclusive notions of Britishness which enables children and young people from all ethnic, cultural and religious backgrounds to affirm their identity as Britons . . . proactively address all forms of discrimination in educational policy and practice, and beyond, to ensure issues such as racism, *sexism and homophobia* are addressed systemically as well as in terms of individual acts of name calling and violence. (2015: 14–15, my emphasis)

We should acknowledge the Swedish government's development of explicit educational policies. It introduced, in 2015, a text for all Swedish sixteen-year-olds: *We Should All Be Feminists* by the African-American writer, Chimamanda Ngozi Adichie (2014). She argues: 'I would also ask that we begin to dream about and plan for a different world. A fairer world. A world of happier men and happier women who are truer to themselves. And this is how to start: we must raise our daughters differently. We must also raise our sons differently . . .' (back cover).

These educational policies and practices are ones that I address, while also adding more explicit consideration of critical feminist educational research from across the globe, to consider fully the ramifications of issues around GRV and education as a tool for transformation. It is based upon what we now know about the relations between men and women in the family and the wider social, political and economic world. Drawing on this knowledge and understanding about how boys' and girls' identities develop, and are shaped by the wider social forces as part of what might now be seen as gender norms or appropriate and acceptable normal social patterns, I set out to show how these could be different, if we were to implement a more equal, fair and respectful education for all.

This also means addressing questions of sexual violence, not just as others' problems or dilemmas but as fundamental to the ongoing relations within British society as much as in other countries of the global North, as well as the global South. While the violent attack in 2012 on Malala for simply arguing in support of girls' education in the Swat Valley of Pakistan has received well-deserved global media attention, this is not simply a problem for countries of the global South (Yousafzai and Lamb 2013). Similarly, the brutal gang rape and murder of a medical student in Delhi, India, in late 2013, has also rightly received enormous public attention, particularly through the showing of the excellent film *India's Daughter* made by Leslee Udeen. Again, this film has been stigmatized as an attack on Indian culture rather than a critique of the ways in which gender norms are deeply embedded in cultures, the exposure of which as an educational technique may be necessary to prevent the continuation of such gendered cultures.

There are many quotidian examples, particularly in the aftermath of the focus on politicians' and celebrities' sexual abuse, emerging almost a decade ago: what is now called 'everyday violence' (for example, the Feminist and Women's Studies Association (FWSA) conference in 2015 was entitled *Encounters with Everyday Violence*). Again, these lead to further stigmatization, and the vilification of young, disadvantaged, vulnerable or fragile women. Discussion has focused on Pakistani or other South Asian men's behaviour, rather than that of men in general. Increasingly, there are also everyday examples of 'lad culture' or 'rape culture' in clubs, on campus or at university and in curricula, as well as in management and leadership in schools and universities (Westmarland 2015).

How the Book is Organized

In the first part of the book, I set the scene for the detailed discussion of work on feminism, sexualities, gender and education that follows in the second part of the book. I reveal the history of feminist scholarship on gender and education and, separately, that of work on campaigning for socio-political and legal changes in the position of women and girls. I also consider international debates from the UN and its educational arm UNESCO about how to effect neoliberal change around gender equality in education. And I look at feminist campaigns for transformations in socio-political and economic contexts, especially across Europe and within individual European countries.

In the second part of the book, I consider how feminism has been at one and the same time a political and an educational project. I demonstrate this through my in-depth study of three generations of academic or education-oriented feminists, and how they learnt reflexively to consider the importance of education in their political activism. I then move on to consider a particular international European feminist project to challenge what we have called GRV amongst children and young people by training educational and youth professionals. This is an imaginative project as it brings together hitherto separate fields of feminist knowledge and activism, namely, education and training on both VAWG and homophobia, with a focus on children and young people.

Drawing on this work, in my concluding chapter I present the outlines of a feminist manifesto for education, arguing for specific and explicit forms of education to challenge traditional gender norms, and indeed the binaries on which they are based, and critiques of forms of sexualities, to ensure a fairer and more equal education for men and women, boys and girls alike. This means going beyond incorporation of these ideas in neoliberalism, and countering its inherent neo-patriarchy or everyday misogyny, to ensure a more progressive and radical agenda to eliminate inequalities and create a fairer, more respectful society.

Part I

*Socio-Cultural and Political
Backgrounds and Contexts*

1

Feminist Research on Gender and Education

Introduction

Here, I set the scene for developing my feminist educational manifesto, by considering the background to current research on gender and education, and women and girls' place within the wider society. This issue is rather more complex than it might appear at first sight. There is much evidence from both academic activist studies and evidence-based policy work for different governments and international organizations in developing or critiquing competitive forms of capitalism. In this chapter, I consider the contested but nuanced feminist research on gender and education, largely conducted in universities. However, the funding, as we shall see, has largely been from organizations that have been committed to policy-relevant research within a neoliberal political framework.

Waves of feminists, from first-wave to second-wave and beyond to the fourth wave of the twenty-first century, have successfully campaigned for women's inclusion in public and political agendas, across the globe. In particular, feminism is no longer a minor political interest, and although the f-word is often reviled, it also frequently appears in popular and social media. The question of its importance on educational agendas is nevertheless contested, particularly around questions of equality, equity, fairness and the future.

The commitment to women's equality has been a complex and contradictory process, from social democratic or socialist agendas to incorporation into liberal processes. Individualism, or 'the selfie generation', has become a hallmark of neoliberalism, resulting in some acceptance of gender equality, while neo-patriarchy, everyday sexism and misogyny continue unabated. This is partly because the social and structural conditions for transformation have not altered, but individual opportunities for enhancement, especially through education, have.

Alison Wolf (2013) celebrates the ways in which middle-class women have been able to succeed as educated women in the labour market, often at the expense of poorer and less fortunate women. Yet others succeed even though they may not have had opportunities for higher education (HE). A particularly important example is how Caitlin Moran has become a feisty feminist journalist and advocate for women despite her lack of university education (Moran 2012).

The proliferation of views about both women or gender and education, broadly conceived, is because of transformations in global capitalism over the last thirty or more years, which have taken on board some of the arguments about gender equality and incorporated them into more marketable versions, evacuating them of more radical meanings. This is what Campbell (2013) and Fraser (2013) argue. What it is to be a woman has led to some contested debates about inclusion or exclusion. In addition, the commercialization or marketization of sex – sometimes referred to as sexualization – has also undermined some of the critiques of traditional categories. Indeed, it is frequently argued now that capitalism is seeping into ever new ways of being, to form more complex traditional social groups and categories. From the point of view of this argument, questions of gender equality can now be debated separately from questions of gender violence, or gender-related violence (GRV), and traditional 'gender norms', or ways of being a woman or a man.

These many versions of feminisms and gender equality include critiques not only of gender norms but also of sexualization, and sexting, through new media, and incorporation into forms and practices of education. Jessica Ringrose and Emma Renold (2012, 2014) have been particularly imaginative in their critique of new social media and have worked with new methodologies around young girls' sexualization, including in primary and secondary schools.

In this chapter, therefore, I want to consider some international evidence regarding gender equality in education by way of illustrating quite how far-reaching these changes have become. I also raise critiques of this international evidence, particularly concerning how this is now part of the neoliberal agenda and not at all transformative in a progressive way.

The development of EU-funded Daphne projects – specifically on women or gender equality and education – is one clear example of the complex and contradictory ways in which these issues have developed in the twenty-first century. Issues about gender equality in education do not necessarily address questions of gender violence, and do not address the transformative potential of education – either in compulsory education or as forms of subsequent training – to deal with the more intractable issues of GRV and cultural traditional gender norms. This is precisely what we aimed to develop through the EU-funded Daphne project.

The development of EU-funded training projects for women as 'victims' of gender violence is a clear example of the complexity of dealing with these issues in changing socio-political times. We wanted to develop some guidelines and tools for starting to question GRV. Thus we wanted to bring together studies of gender equality and of GRV, with the explicit objective of trying to transform future generations of children's lives. We were also explicit about using traditional feminist activist theories to achieve these objectives. I will therefore return to discuss our aims and approach, having set the broader international context of complex questions of gender equality in education.

Feminist Values and Demands for Women's Liberation

I draw on how feminism has become not only a political and social movement for change, but also a part of academic life, developing knowledge and scholarship to facilitate the processes of progressive changes. It has, in other words, become an educational movement, as evidence from my study about waves of feminist activists in universities illustrates (David 2014). First-wave feminism in the UK as elsewhere was about political and economic change, with a key focus on women's suffrage (Banks 1986). Very few of the British first-wave feminists that Banks studied were involved in university education, inevitably perhaps given their exclusion from full participation as students.

Second-wave feminism has entailed more detailed analysis of the factors that might inhibit wider change, through cultures and social systems. This is in part to do with the growth of feminism alongside the growth of HE. While these two processes have developed together, feminism is largely in tandem with HE, rather than in parallel or as an integral part. Indeed, education remains resistant to incorporating feminist values as a central component.

There have been major transformations both in the economy and in the role which HE plays in relation to economic growth from the twentieth to the twenty-first centuries, which is now known as academic capitalism (Slaughter and Leslie 1997; Slaughter and Rhoades 2004). These transformations have led to women's greater involvement in both economic or work activities and in education, including HE. Nevertheless, the developments have been uneven and unevenly spread across social groups and institutions.

It remains the case that women, including those in academia, remain in relatively subordinate positions to men, despite all the changes (Morley 2013). Moreover, male power has become more resistant and resilient to change. In its new form it has variously been called patriarchy and sexism (Lerner 1986; Mackay 2015).

Yet feminism as a form of political activism and as a set of theoretical and conceptual tools is firmly embedded within the academy.

In the 1960s, as part of civil, human rights and social movements, women's liberation was linked to campaigns for greater civic and social equality. The majority of early campaigns were drawn from international student social movements around welfare and human rights. Inevitably these movements took various forms of liberal or social democracy in the countries where they were based. Such movements were usually contested (Mackay 2015).

As a result of much campaigning and debate, 1970 proved, with the benefit of hindsight, to be a critical year for articulating new arguments about sexual equality, leading to what could be seen as *a manifesto for women's liberation*. It was the year in which major seminal or ovarian publications came out in the global North: for example, Shulamith Firestone's *The Dialectic of Sex,* Eva Figes' *Patriarchal Attitudes,* Germaine Greer's *The Female Eunuch,* and Kate Millett's *Sexual Politics.* They provided critiques of the contemporary situation written by women, as students, in HE in the UK or the US.

They were not the first such texts, as Simone de Beauvoir's *The Second Sex* had been published more than ten years earlier in France; and Betty Friedan's *The Feminine Mystique,* published in 1963 in the US, about married women graduates living with 'the problem that has no name', had launched the National Organization for Women (NOW) in the US.

In the UK, the first women's liberation movement (WLM) conference was held in 1970 at Ruskin College, Oxford, a working-men's college loosely linked to the university. This had been organized by [graduate] students, including the redoubtable Sheila Rowbotham who subsequently published *Women, Resistance and Revolution* (1972), *Hidden from History* (1973a) and *Women's Consciousness, Man's World* (1973b). The conference aimed to develop *a manifesto of demands on the state* for sexual equality and social change. Over the next few years of the 1970s, those demands became the principles and values of the women's movement, based as they became on growing social and historical research, carried out within and beyond the academy.

It was during this era of social welfare that women entered the academy in increasing numbers, as students, academics and researchers, beginning the processes of gathering systematic socio-historical evidence. This gradually became feminist scholarship and knowledge, slowly but surely becoming known as 'the feminist canon' (Davis and Evans 2011).

Indeed, these early movements are now known as 'second-wave feminism' to distinguish them from the 'first-wave feminism' of the nineteenth and early twentieth centuries, which were largely campaigns for political suffrage and economic independence. Mackay (2015) assumes that second-wave feminism had its origins in these movements, although she does not emphasize involvement in HE, focusing on activism. But her own research on feminists for her doctorate is the basis for *Radical Feminism: Feminist Activism in Movement*.

The initial four 'demands' of the British WLM were: equal educational opportunities; equal pay for equal work; contraception and abortion on demand; and twenty-four-hour day nurseries. Legal and financial independence, a right to define one's own sexuality and elimination of violence against women were quickly added as the fifth, sixth and seventh demands (Coote and Campbell 1982). While none of these 'demands' have been fully met, understanding why there has been such resistance to change has become an important aspect of developing feminist scholarship and knowledge, including around understanding the role of social psyches, and the unconscious.

I will return, in the concluding chapter, to consider the elements of such a set of demands or manifesto today, looking at the array of feminist manifestos, from UKFeminista to Everyday Sexism to WOW (Women of the World), and other more education- and/or sexually focused questions. This will include returning to the important points made by the British Labour Party's *Manifesto for Women*, and the WE Party. These are all issues that have been raised in the twenty-first century, particularly with the resurgence of feminism, and its new but contested political activism.

The Emergence and Evolution of Feminist Knowledge and Understanding

Susie Orbach and Luise Eichenbaum founded the Women's Therapy Centre (WTC) in London in 1976, based upon a psycho-therapeutic understanding of women's lives, to provide support for all women in achieving a greater understanding of their inner lives. Orbach's (1978) best-selling *Fat is a Feminist Issue (Fifi)* was then published to critical acclaim, remaining a key text about women's sensibilities, and spawning critical approaches to our understandings of sexual relations.

In 2013, Orbach with Lisa Appignanesi and Rachel Holmes produced an edited collection entitled *Fifty Shades of Feminism* (2013), illustrating feminism's broad appeal. The title borrowed from a best-selling salacious novel published in 2012 about BDSM (Bondage, Discipline, Sado-Masochism) – *Fifty Shades of Grey* – written by a woman, E. L. James, addressing a young woman's fantasies about her intimate sexual relations with men. Interestingly, she reverted to the traditional habit of not revealing her forenames, perhaps illustrating the ongoing sexist subordinate position of women, in intimate sexual life too. But the woman narrator was highly educated and sophisticated, graduating from university as the novel opened.

Many feminists have argued that the book contributes to 'mommy porn' or more specifically reflects today's GRV. Appignanesi argued that 'fifty million women readers can't be altogether wrong . . . [but] our times are still embroiled in misogyny . . . so it is 50 women exploring what feminism means today' (2013: 38).

This illustrates the paradoxical nature of the publicity afforded feminism in the media, combined with the fact of women's intimate, sexual and social position remaining subordinate and subject to violence. A sequel has recently been published (James 2015) from the man's perspective, illustrating how violence may be endemic in male fantasies about intimate heterosexual relations. Indeed, if these were not merely fantasies they would be subject to the criminal law.

During the 1970s, as more women students entered HE, new explicitly feminist courses and pedagogies developed apace. As there was very little material on which to base our course studies, inevitably we had to develop our own materials for a variety of courses around women's studies and emerging critiques of sexual relations (for example, Bristol Women's Studies Group (BWSG) 1978).

Given the evolving nature of academic life, opportunities for developing our own courses and materials emerged. For example, *The State, The Family and Education* (David 2015a) was published originally in 1980, based upon our innovative work for an under-graduate course in 'family and social policy', taught jointly with feminist colleagues Hilary Land (1976) and Jackie West (1980). We did not have a blueprint for what we should teach, but drew on various theories or concepts known to us from our own learning. We all tried to provide materials about the historical developments of relations between men and women in the family and the wider society, including the economy and the developing range of social and welfare services.

I concentrated on how women's education had emerged from medieval times and what its relation to women, the family and state had been. It contributed to important and innovative developments in feminist knowledge and was vital for feminist campaigning for equal educational opportunities. As an emerging feminist, and also a socialist, I fell upon the French Marxist philosopher Louis Althusser's notion of the 'family-education couple' as one of what he called 'ideological state apparatuses', as a way to illustrate and conceptualize the linkages. These ideas may seem very out-of-date now, especially in the borrowing from a Marxian man, but at that time they were useful ways of rendering visible what had been obscured by generations of scholarship that ignored the specificities of women's work and roles in the family and schooling.

I undertook a historical analysis of how teachers, mothers and daughters had been treated in terms of rights and responsibilities up to contemporary times in the UK, although I did not tease out many of the four country-specific differences. As I saw it at the time, this book was but one contribution to the building of feminist knowledge or emerging historical scholarship on which to base future political and pedagogical practices.

The resurgence of feminism and attention to women's rights in the twenty-first century, as both a political and an educational movement, means that our collective work of academic activism is not yet accomplished, despite the subsequent generations of manifold scholarship and pedagogical practices. Equal opportunities for women and girls have still not been realized as male power, patriarchy and misogyny retain a stranglehold over education and the rest of society. The fact that this text has been republished illustrates its renewed relevance. The book remains one vital contribution to our understanding of social and sexual divisions and relations; divisions that are highlighted today in a world where sexual abuse remains an urgent social problem.

Nevertheless, it also means that although there have been important changes in women's lives, to which feminists have surely contributed, a historical understanding is required of what still needs to be done, or even what needs to be undone and refashioned for a fairer and more respectful education. There have been important changes to women's economic, educational and family lives, but we have moved away from a social democratic model of governance to a more individualistic and neoliberal system. While there has been an enormous amount of feminist historical, sociological and educational scholarship in the last forty years, it is still the case that it is largely ignored in the mainstream (or what Mary O'Brien (1981) called 'the malestream'). It is some of this scholarship that I present.

Gender and Education as a Field of Feminist Research

From the explosion of international work on gender and education over the last thirty-five years, important contributions both to policies or practices and to developments in feminist knowledge have emerged. The creation in the UK of the journal *Gender and*

Education was particularly important in developing and systematiz-
ing knowledge of and approaches to the field, such that there is an
enormous range now available to draw upon. This is intellectually
and empirically rich, and highly controversial.

The focus upon recent scholarship and research is in no way
intended to diminish our understandings of the work of feminist
scholars, especially in developing women's educational history,
drawing on the insights of the social sciences such as those of Carol
Dyhouse, Gerda Lerner, June Purvis and our own early studies in
the sociology of education. The importance of the early scholarship
of Banks (1985, 1986) in both developing a feminist understanding
of waves of feminism, especially of the first wave, and creating the
field of the sociology of education is crucial.

From the 1970s, however, feminist research around gender and
education also began to mushroom. This focused more squarely
on girls' equal educational treatment and achievements, largely
ignoring the question of violence. For example, feminist studies
began to emerge, such as Deem's (1978) *Women and Schooling* and
Byrne's (1978) *Women and Education*. Other early work of particular note includes the three British school-based books entitled
The Gender Trap: A Closer Look at Sex Roles, by the late Carol
Adams, with Rae Laurikietis and Andy Johnson, first published
in 1976.

The late Sue Lees was particularly important for how she considered girls' developing identities in relation to schooling and the
wider society in, first, *Losing Out: Sexuality and Adolescent Girls*
(1986), now recognised as seminal, followed by *Sugar and Spice:
Sexuality and Adolescent Girls* (1993). Similarly, Valerie Walkerdine
has been influential for her psycho-social studies, *Counting Girls
Out* (1998) and *Schoolgirl Fictions* (1990), while Val Hey's (1997)
The Company She Keeps has been particularly salient in developing
our understandings of schoolgirl friendships.

But much of this early second-wave feminist work did not
have much traction within the social sciences. It did, however,
have some influence upon the developing theoretical frameworks,
particularly with the increasing uses of the concept of gender as
distinctive from sexual divisions. It was important to campaigning

around gender-equality policies, oriented as it was to social and educational change, based on social-scientific evidence.

Such was the growth of this scholarship that the UK Equal Opportunities Commission (EOC), founded in 1975, began to fund studies of contemporary girls' schooling. By the end of the twentieth century, there was a veritable melange of studies. Arnot, David and Weiner (1996, 1999) were commissioned by the EOC to undertake a study of the impact of changing policies and practices in secondary schools. Using mixed methods, we studied the myriad of changes in schooling with statistical evidence from national examination results and qualitative evidence from schools. We reported to the EOC (Arnot et al. 1996), presaging future work in the twenty-first century.

By the time we came to publish our study, the language and discourse of educational research had shifted to those of gender equality and the question of gender gaps. Entitling our study *Closing the Gender Gap: Postwar Education and Social Change* (Arnot et al. 1999), we reported that, on the evidence of examination results, there had been an inexorable shift towards gender equality in schooling. We concluded rather melodramatically:

> The school system has made various ambivalent responses to the[se] processes of social change . . . Retaining a sense of continuity with the past is the function of school systems, since schooling contributes to the moral order as well as catering to the vicissitudes of the occupational structure. But in the UK, schooling appears to have broken with the traditions of the gender order. It is this decisive break with the social and educational past that lies behind the closing of the gender gap. (1999: 156)

With the benefit of hindsight, we did not fully consider the ways in which the links between schooling and the moral order were being retained in subtle ways and in definitions of what it is to be a girl or a boy, and how this is maintained. But giving consideration to the gender order, or the maintenance of 'gender norms' that establishes ways of being men and women, is even more complex than we had then considered. We were concerned about how to achieve educational equality in terms of success within examinations and across a range of school subjects or disciplines. We did not fully consider the ramifications of socio-cultural change, linked with neoliberal economic developments.

The Biographic, Post-Structural Turn in Education and Social Sciences

There were strong academic debates, in which many second-wave education feminists participated, which led these ideas to be seen as a turn in methodologies and philosophical approaches. These developments across the arts, humanities and social sciences were often viewed as moving towards a 'biographic turn'. While heavily contested, the debates centred upon notions of the centrality of social structures as opposed to agency and identity. These hinged upon, in brief, the issues about whether this turn led away from structuralism towards post-structuralism, on the one hand, and, on the other, methodological debates about the nature of realism, with critical realism becoming ascendant.

There is no question of the American feminist Judith Butler's intellectual impact on the field, originating from her major study, *Gender Trouble: Feminism and the Subversion of Identity*, published in 1990. This was a study of the philosophical underpinnings to the concepts of sex and gender, drawing especially on French philosophy and psychoanalysis, including consideration of Simone de Beauvoir and Michel Foucault. She argued, most importantly, against the notion of theoretical binaries and for the notion of the performative. In this work, she coined the concepts of 'heterosexual matrix' and 'queer theory'.

Similarly, Margaret Archer as a sociologist of education not of the feminist persuasion has had a growing influence, more recently on methodological approaches and the uses of critical realism by contrast with post-structural approaches. Her earlier work was an attempt to develop and systematize educational systems.

Collections on Gender and Education

One way in which the field has been developed has been through a series of edited collections. Initially the British second-wave feminists, Madeleine Arnot and Gaby Weiner, put together two important collections, one entitled *Gender and the Politics of Schooling* (Arnot and Weiner 1987), followed by Weiner and Arnot (1987), *Gender under Scrutiny: New Inquiries in Education.* Both were seen to provide evidence of the state of the field. Their focus was centrally about the forms and effects of schooling, and especially secondary schooling, upon girls and their developments and achievements. This was linked broadly to the changing policy frameworks and the pursuit of equal opportunities for girls with boys.

Similarly, the American second-wave feminist, Catherine Marshall (1997a, b), gathered together collections of evidence of the international field in a pair of edited books entitled *Feminist Critical Policy Analysis I* and *II.* These two collections focused particularly on the ways in which the development of feminist scholarship was contributing to policy change within the wider educational systems and society.

Little attention was paid, however, to what remained relatively hidden issues of sexual abuse, bullying and harassment or stereotyping amongst peer groups or between adults and children. These remained outside the orbit of this kind of educational or social research. Such studies tend to be conducted in a separate sphere of psycho-social studies or studies of women and children within families, where Liz Kelly (1988) had a singularly vital influence.

In the twenty-first century, such has been the growth of the field of scholarship that many more international collections and encyclopedias have been produced. Barbara Bank (2007), with Sara Delamont and Catherine Marshall, put together an important two-volume encyclopedia of *Gender and Education.* These two volumes range widely across the fields of endeavour from elaborating the gendered theories of education, through gender issues in educational research and institutional contexts for gendered education, to gendered constructions and achievements in the official and hidden curricula, the extra-curriculum and the peer group. Gendered teaching and administration and gender and educational policies are also considered, here with a particular emphasis on issues to do with sexual harassment policies and equity legislation. They illustrate the growing importance of issues to do with gender equality, entwined with gender-based or gender-related violence.

Bank has also extended her analysis of gender and education from schooling into higher education, in *Gender and Higher Education* (2011), where she gives consideration to how the field is developing, with theoretical perspectives and educational research, institutional structures and contexts, gender constructions and controversies in the academic and extra-curricula, gendered faculty and administration, again ending with gender and higher-education policies, including sexual harassment.

Two of the editors of *Gender and Education* – Christine Skelton and Becky Francis – also produced an overview of the contributions to the field, together with Lisa Smulyan, through the *SAGE Handbook of Gender & Education* (2006). This volume has been described as 'a theoretically sophisticated collection of chapters by leading figures in the international field of gender and education . . . captures the broadening focus of research and theory in gender and education, offering a wide range and diversity of voices and topics . . . considerations of gender have become central in educational theory and policy' (Kathleen Weiler 1988), and as 'compelling reading for anyone (practitioner, policy-maker, school teacher, academic or university student) interested in pursuing current debates in the field' (Rosemary Deem 1978). What is particularly important about this volume is the new emphasis on gender, race and class within primary or elementary classrooms, as well as secondary schools, and on young people's emergent identities, and linked to international issues in educational development.

Such is the strength of the field now that Weaver-Hightower and Skelton (2013) invited contributions to a volume entitled *Leaders in Gender and Education: Intellectual Self-Portraits*. The seventeen international contributors were all asked to assess their unique work in developing the field, with over a third of the contributors being male pro-feminists, rather than feminists per se. A small number also addressed the question of how the field was developing in the US, around policies and school practices, addressing sexualities and homophobia.

Women Interrupting, Disrupting, and Revolutionising Educational Policy and Practice, edited by Whitney Sherman Newcomb and Katherine Cumings Mansfield (2014), is also of importance. This volume uses the insights of second-wave feminist research to inform current practices and look to the future for feminist and gender research, particularly around leadership. Theirs is a particularly useful focus on the intersections of class, ethnicity or race and gender in developing concerns about how to take forward issues around gender and sexuality. They make a special plea for the importance of gender and sexuality in teacher preparation, and in professional developments around youth and community activism.

The American feminist teacher blogger Ileana Jimenez has been particularly assiduous in promoting these issues as an activist teacher in high schools in the US for the last decade. Her work has focused especially on using feminist literature for embedding the insights of research into the gender consciousness of young people.

All of these considerations are particularly important in recent feminist research, especially the work of, for instance, Marianne Bloch (2003) and colleagues, bringing together international work on reconceptualizing early childhood education; Claire Maxwell with Peter Aggleton (2013) on boys' and girls' identities; Emma Renold on primary classrooms and children, and, with Ringrose (2012), on feminisms in school, and on sexting and other social media creating sexualization. Similarly, Ringrose's questioning of the recent policy debates about the success of gender equality in education in *Post-Feminist Education?* (2012), has been particularly important. There has also been sophisticated work on how policy and practices have influenced changing concepts of femininities, such as work on black girls (Mirza 1992; Brah and Phoenix 2004), and Farzana Shain (2011) has paid attention to the impacts of recent political issues on Muslim boys.

Gender, Violence and Education

One important aspect of this work, which was until the twenty-first century obscured, concerns what was earlier called domestic, sexual or spousal violence. In the 1970s, second-wave feminists pioneered the establishment of what became known as women's refuges in the UK, and women's shelters in North America. In the UK, the women's aid movement began to establish places of rescue for women as victims of male violence and to analyse the process (Kelly 1988; Hamner and Saunders 1977; Greenan 2005).

Erin Pizzey's (1973) *Scream Quietly or the Neighbours Will Hear* was published to critical acclaim in the UK, and taken up in the British Parliament, although it has also been derided. The title itself illustrates just how hidden and secretive an issue this was, and how difficult it remains to provide an adequate name for such sexual and physical violence. From the 1970s, some community organizations and local authorities began to fund and provide alternative housing for women, especially those with children, to escape their violent partners. This movement also became an international one, and was highly effective in European communities.

Given the difficulties with naming the issues, how much more so has been the issue of child abuse, whether about bullying, sexual violence, or paedophilia and child sexual exploitation (Kelly 1988). Back in the 1970s, there was little official recognition of the kinds of sexual abuse and violence against young children (Jackson 1982). Indeed, the fine line or distinction between abuse, bullying and acceptable adult violence towards children was frequently debated.

On the one hand, the traditions of public-school punishments were exposed as cruel, and some argued that children should be given the same rights as adults (Alderson and Morrow 1995; Alderson 2000), whereas others argued for forms of child protection. Debates also began to emerge on the age of sexual consent and around teenage parenthoods (Allen 2001; Epstein and Johnson 1998; Kelly 2001; Luttrell 2003; Pillow 2004).

Together with Pam Alldred (2007), I undertook a study of the nuanced forms of gender and sexual relations. In *Get Real About Sex: The Politics and Practice of Sex Education*, we looked at how issues around the moral and gender order and sexual relations were taught in contemporary schooling. We focused on young people's attitudes to sex and to sex and relationship education (SRE), as well as on how teachers and other professionals approach and feel regarding teaching about these intimate social and sexual relations.

We found that such teachers feel inadequate to the question, especially without training and advice. And yet they are still not trained specifically to teach or deal with issues around gender relations, the history of these changing processes, or about current issues concerning bullying, sexual harassment and other forms of GRV. Moreover, there is nothing in the formal school curriculum or in the governance of schools that attends to questions of sexual consent. We were made crucially aware of how it is not only the formal school curriculum that helps boys and girls learn, but also the informal and the organization of school governance and practices, including, for example, mothers' versus fathers' responsibilities for the daily practices of schooling.

We concluded that:

> We make a plea for a more compassionate schooling that values relationships above all and that therefore questions the reliance on market forces to improve education. A supportive environment would allow committed educators to facilitate young people to see themselves as sexual subjects, to recognize the pressures of a culture awash with profit-driven sexual imagery, and to resist the extension of capitalist logic to emotional and sexual relationships. Students learn from the culture of a school as much as from curriculum content. Schools are delivering their most powerful lessons about relationships and sexuality in the degree to which they respect the diverse bodies, desires and emotions of both teachers and pupils. The real challenge in schools lies in the practice of compassionate relationships that are both sustaining and sustainable. (Alldred and David 2007: 191)

It is this study, and other work around gender equality and gender violence, and the continuing lack of SRE or personal, social and health education (PSHE) in schools, that led us to consider a wider European context for the study of how to challenge forms of GRV against and by children and young people. What could we learn from the experiences of others and especially from feminist pedagogues in other countries?

EU Daphne Programmes on Gender and Sexual Violence

The EU launched the Daphne Initiative in May 1997, as an one-year funding line of 3 million ecus to fund non-governmental organizations (NGOs) for projects that support victims of violence and combat violence against women and girls (VAWG). It was created by the European Commission (EC) as a response to the events of 1996 that had shaken Europe and galvanized public and political opinion.

The discovery of the bodies of a number of missing girls in premises in Belgium in late summer 1996 raised questions about what Europe could do to protect children and women from those who wished to abuse or exploit them for profit. The one-year Daphne Initiative of 1997 struck a chord with NGOs and response to the two calls for proposals was high, with assessors led by the redoubtable Professor Liz Kelly, from the UK. (She is head of the Child and Women's Abuse Unit at London Metropolitan University.)

As a result, funding for the initiative was renewed in 1998 (increased to 5 million ecus) and in 1999. The Daphne Programme (2000–3) continued the work of the initiative, with funding of 20 million euros over four years, followed by Daphne II (2004–6) with an average annual budget of 10 million euros, and then by the Daphne III (2007–13) with an average annual budget of 16.7 million euros. The Daphne programme continues in the period 2014–20, as one part of the Rights, Equality and Citizenship Programme of the EU. Our GAP project was funded under the Daphne III programme, which was to provide training and education for professionals.

Aims and Methods of our GAP Project

This project was designed and coordinated by a group of feminist and critical educators and researchers, to develop training and pedagogical tools for practitioners who have everyday contact with general populations of children and young people ('youth practitioners'). Pam Alldred (Brunel University), the principal investigator, had a background in SRE (sex or sexualities and relationships education), meaning that norm-critical pedagogies were influences on the project design (Bromseth 2010). Pam had met Barbara Biglia, based at Universitat Rovira I Virgili (URV) in Tarragona, Spain, through critical psychology and feminist activism sharing a commitment to not individualizing social problems. Alldred, Cullen and David were also colleagues through the Gender and Education Association (GEA) and as professional educators (Cullen 2013).

Pam brought together twenty partners or associate partners in six countries in Europe to challenge GRV against (and by) children and young people. These teams were made up of a mix of feminist academics and professionals in NGOs, in areas relevant to professional education and training. While the overarching project involved partners based in six countries who were involved in developing the analytical and theoretical components of the research, only four countries developed particular actions, through feminist academic practice as pilot schemes.

Each of the four partner countries designed and delivered new training for practitioners (their ACTION), and the training aims were both *responsive* and *preventative*: that is, through improved knowledge and understanding youth practitioners would be better able to, first, identify and challenge sexist, sexualizing, homophobic or controlling language and behaviour, and, second, support children and young people (CYP), and know when and how to refer to the most appropriate support services.

In addition, the project explicitly builds on two influential previous projects that members have been involved in: the EU-FRC co-funded AHEAD (Against Homophobia: European

Local Administration Devices) project, which mapped good practice in EU countries in tackling homo/transphobia and evaluated
a City of Turin Pride Office training course (Coll-Planas et al.
2011), and the UK-based, 2006–9 ESRC-funded No Outsiders
project, which made a range of educational interventions to challenge hetero-normativity in primary schools (Atkinson et al. 2009).

The definition of GRV is of relatively recent origin, dating
back to the last decade of the twentieth century. This was an
attempt to go beyond the official UN and EU definitions, seen as
rather anodyne. In 1993, El-Bushra and Pisa Lopez defined GRV
as 'violence which embodies the power imbalance inherent in
a patriarchal society' and explained that this is overwhelmingly,
though not necessarily, carried out by men against women. Over
the intervening years terminology has altered, but what we wish to
maintain in this definition is its plurality and socio-cultural analysis.
This plurality is needed in order to recognize fully the differential
impact of intersectionality and power structures on socio-histori-
cally positioned individuals. At the social level of analysis, this is
to problematize the social norms, tolerance and silences around
violence and around gender more generally.

By 2012, the term 'gender-based violence' (GBV) was used
more frequently than GRV. For example, the European Institute
for Gender Equality (EIGE) said: 'GBV is violence that is directed
against a person on the basis of gender'. So, if GBV is violence that is
fundamentally created or allowed by gender inequality, GRV might
be defined more broadly to incorporate and acknowledge other
forms of inequality (Alldred and David 2015: 15; Mackay 2015).

This broad concept is compatible with feminist approaches
that problematize all inequalities and attend to power differentials
across all forms of social difference (race, ethnicity, class, gender,
sexual orientation), and with social theory that emphasizes the
intersectionality of gender with class and ethnicity (Anthias and
Yuval-Davis 1993: Brah 1992). Indeed, problematizing the gender
binary and gender and sexual normativities reflects the broader
deconstructive move of third-wave or postmodern feminism and
of queer theory in particular. Butler's (1993) articulation of the
heterosexual matrix's mutual constitution through the gender

binary is a key influence in the project's challenge to hetero-normativity (Alldred and David 2015).

Overall, we considered that, given feminist and critical knowledge, we could work with some other professionals and practitioners to pilot and develop materials for working with children and young people in educational or 'training' settings. We knew that professionals outside legal or welfare services typically have little training about how to deal with gender violence. We therefore designed our project to address the EU Daphne-III priority of *the preparation and delivery of training to professionals in contact with victims* and made an ongoing intervention in practitioners' knowledge and skills. We wanted to leave a legacy of lasting resources for practitioners, and therefore trained skills-sharing practitioners in four countries.

Our definition of violence (Alldred and David 2015: 15) includes GBV but covers a wider terrain. This breadth of definition allowed us to put *gender norms and normativity* at the centre. It enabled us to draw together two strands of activism in Western Europe that, for the most part, have been separate in recent history: efforts to challenge violence against women and girls, and efforts to tackle homophobia. This tests the thesis that problematizing gender norms challenges values and norms underpinning both these forms of oppression.

The overall goal of the project was to improve the way professionals who have general contact with children and young people recognize GRV, intervene to challenge it (and the values that underpin it), and refer on individuals affected. The specific objectives were fourfold:

> *Training:* to design innovative, tailored training to help practitioners recognize and challenge a broad range of GRV among CYP, and increase their knowledge of the position of CYP regarding the law and support services, and so refer them appropriately and to deliver this as additional training to 200 various youth practitioners in each country.
>
> *Research:* to evaluate the training provided at Local Action level and collate information from NGOs on GRV training and

evaluation to build up European experience and international knowledge; to compare the policy situation about GRV for young people across Europe and to conduct a joint evaluation of the local actions to identify success factors and obstacles to effective GRV training.

Legacy: to develop and pilot new information aimed at youth practitioners in each site; to make resources widely available to practitioners or professional bodies; and to support trainees in sharing their learning.

Dissemination: to publish findings in home languages and cultures and to share learning with other academics, providers of professional training and education, policymakers and others. (Adapted from Alldred and David 2015: 10)

However, our project worked across different professional groups in the four countries in which we were working, although all were concerned to develop methods to challenge GRV amongst children and young people. At the outset, we all agreed that it would be through improved knowledge and understanding that 'youth practitioners' could better identify and challenge sexist, sexualizing, homophobic or controlling language and behaviour, and know when and how to refer children and young people to the most appropriate support services.

Our definitions of GRV in a broad educational context meant that we also incorporated a range of issues related to gender equality, and to challenging sexism and sexualization, including forms of homophobia. We were concerned to challenge traditional 'gender norms' that pigeon-holed particular categories of girls and boys. We took a post-structural approach to what has been called the 'gender matrix'.

The overall aims of the project across all the four countries in which we worked were to *bridge the gaps* in practice between: support services for adults and for children, specialist victim-support services and everyday professional contact, supporting those affected and intervening to challenge or pre-empt violence, and, finally, actions focused on dating violence or on homophobia.

This fourth 'gap' is the reason that a broad definition of GRV is adopted, which problematizes *sexist, sexualizing or norm-driven bullying and harassment, whichever children and young people are targeted.* The rationale was that placing a critique of gender normativity at the centre might simultaneously undermine violence against women and girls, homophobic, lesbophobic *and* transphobic or gender-norm-related violence.

To bridge these gaps, the project planned the mutual education of training partners, which were victim-support community services, and trainees (youth practitioners). The aims of our training of practitioners were to improve their knowledge of support organizations and legislation, and hence, first, their effective referring and, secondly, their ability to challenge violent or discriminatory language and behaviour, thereby contributing to the development of a protective environment for children, young people and women.

Conclusions

I have laid out the broad field of research and policy-based evidence on gender and education, developing from social democracy and social movements, including feminism. I turn now to consider some of the ways that the field has been captured by a neoliberal approach to gender equality in education through international organizations, followed by consideration of feminist campaigns for legal and social changes internationally.

2

Political Changes on Gender Equality in Education

Introduction:
Changing International Organizations

There have been extensive international socio-economic and political changes in the last century around the incorporation of women's rights and responsibilities within socio-legal discourse, as a result of feminist and women's campaigning. Yet patriarchal or sexist relations remain. Indeed, they are exacerbated by a focus upon an increasingly individualized and yet globalized economy of neoliberalism.

Gender equality as a concept has replaced that of sexual or women's equality. It is now threaded through British, European and international policies and legislation, in ways previously unknown. Nevertheless, gender equality as a concept does not always embrace issues around forms of violence against women (VAW). Indeed, these notions have also developed unevenly through the vagaries of changing global political contexts. I shall briefly address these changing global developments here by way of context to what follows.

Up to the nineteenth century, across the globe, women were economically, politically and socially subordinate to men. Nevertheless, 'first-wave feminists' struggled to achieve major changes in industrializing countries of the global North, such that, by the early twentieth century, campaigns for women's suffrage were beginning to be successful. With this achievement, in many of these countries there was a period of quiescence during which feminists struggled for other, more radical change.

At the end of the Second World War, however, and through the creation of the United Nations (UN) in 1945, there were further moves to try to embed civil and human rights, including women's rights. Of the original fifty-one member states, only thirty allowed women equal voting rights with men or permitted them to hold public office. Nevertheless, the drafters of the United Nations Charter, including Eleanor Roosevelt – then the 'first lady' of the US – deliberately referred to the 'equal rights of men and women' (David 2014: 27). The Universal Declaration of Human Rights declared the UN's 'faith in fundamental human rights' and the 'dignity and worth of the human person'.

No previous international legal document had so forcefully affirmed the equality of all human beings or specifically targeted sex as a basis for discrimination. Roosevelt became the first chair of the UN Commission on Human Rights in the late 1940s and later, in the 1960s, she chaired the Kennedy Administration's US Presidential Commission on the Status of Women.

The UN: From Sexual to Gender Equality

During the first three decades, the UN's work on behalf of women focused primarily on the codification of women's legal and civil rights, and the gathering of data on the status of women around the world. It became increasingly apparent that laws, in and of themselves, were not enough to ensure the equal rights of women.

As a result of women's campaigning and pressure groups, from the 1970s, there developed four UN world conferences on women, the first one being held in Mexico City in 1975. This led to the establishment of the International Research and Training Institute for the Advancement of Women (INSTRAW) and the United Nations Development Fund for Women (UNIFEM) to provide the institutional framework for research, training and operational activities in the area of women and development. The second conference was held in Copenhagen, in 1980, and the third in Nairobi in 1985.

Hillary Clinton, then first lady of the US, made a strong plea for more commitment to women's rights at the fourth UN world conference in Beijing in 1995. The four conferences united the international community behind a set of common objectives with an effective plan of action for the advancement of women everywhere, in all spheres of public and private life.

The struggle for women's equality shifted towards gender equality in this second phase, from regarding women almost exclusively in terms of their development needs, to recognizing their essential contributions to the entire development process, to seeking their empowerment and the promotion of their right to full participation at all levels of human activity.

In December 1979, the UN General Assembly adopted the Convention on the Elimination of All Forms of Discrimination Against Women (CEDAW), termed 'the bill of rights for women'. This now legally binds 165 states and obligates them to report within one year of ratification, and subsequently every four years, on the steps they have taken to remove obstacles they face in implementing the Convention. (At the same time the UN also passed a path-breaking Convention on the Rights of the Child.)

VAW was defined as physical, sexual or psychological violence against women because of their sex alone or where such violence affects women disproportionately (Mackay 2015: 9–10). By the 1990s, pressures for women's rights and issues around VAWG were such that the UN considered the issue. In Article 1 of the UN Declaration on the Elimination of Violence against Women (DEVAW), proclaimed by the UN General Assembly in its Resolution 48/104 of 20 December 1993, it defined the term 'VAW' as: 'Any act of gender-based violence that results in, or is likely to result in, physical, sexual or psychological harm or suffering to women, including threats of such acts, coercion or arbitrary deprivation of liberty, whether occurring in public or in private life' (A/RES/48/104, 20 Dec. 1993, of the UN General Assembly).

The UN also created UNESCO – the UN Educational, Scientific and Cultural Organization – to develop its data and policies around these social questions. UNESCO now includes working with the Organization for Economic Cooperation and Development (OECD) and the World Bank. Linked to these organizations is also the World Health Organization (WHO). In addition, it entails working with European countries grouped together through the EU. However, there are contradictions between the ways in which women's and gender equality and violence are defined and treated.

The WHO definition of violence also omits recognition of structural and cultural forms (WHO 2002). We find its understanding too individualized and volitional: as feminist educators and researchers, we wanted an approach that helps to demonstrate the links between different forms of violence and between violence and power relations, and that foregrounds the political analysis of violence (Alldred and David 2015).

UNESCO, Global Feminism and Education

There was also a series of UN-organized world conferences on education, which linked together women's rights and which became known as 'global feminism'. At the 1990 first UN World Conference on Education for All, held in Jomtien, Thailand, representatives from 155 countries launched the Education for All (EFA) movement by agreeing to make primary education accessible to all children and to reduce illiteracy by the end of the decade.

EFA meant educating both boys and girls and considered the treating of both sexes equally – and in the process narrowing the 'gender gap' – to be a matter of justice and equality. Jomtien marked the beginning of intensified international support for assuring access to quality education for girls, a cause that was reaffirmed ten years later at the World Education Forum in Dakar, Senegal, with participants from 164 countries.

Another important development was the signing, in September 2000, of a UN Millennium Declaration by all 192 UN member states and at least twenty-three international organizations, which laid out a set of Millennium Development Goals (MDGs) to be reached by 2015. It was here that the term 'gender equality' became accepted into official legal and international discussions.

> *A closely related theme running through all of these discussions has been that of gender equality in education.* From the outset, the global community has recognized that educating girls and women is an imperative, not only as a matter of respecting a basic human right for half the population but as a powerful and necessary first step to achieving the broader goals of EFA ... following the landmark Fourth World Conference on Women held in Beijing in September 1995, attended by representatives of 189 governments and 2,100 non-governmental organizations, the international community reached a consensus on achieving gender equality in education. (UNESCO 2012: 8; my emphasis)

UNESCO therefore set out to monitor this process of achieving gender equality in education by 2015, and to investigate gender progress and gaps. It produced a *World Atlas on Gender Equality in Education* in 2012, arguing that: 'This Atlas is a map of the world; *it is also a call to action, to concentrate ever more on promoting gender equality in education as a human right and a development multiplier*' (2012: 1; my emphasis). It also developed a sophisticated take on the differences between gender equality and gender parity:

> Traditionally, all societies have given preference to males over females when it comes to educational opportunity, and disparities in educational attainment and literacy rates today reflect patterns which have been shaped by the social and education policies and practices of the past. As a result, virtually all countries face gender disparities of some sort. Given the strong correlations that exist between GDP and educational attainment, all countries have incentives to make the best possible use of all of their human resources. In discussing education

and gender it is helpful to distinguish between 'gender parity' and 'gender equality'.

Gender parity aims at achieving equal participation for girls and boys in education. Gender equality is understood more broadly as the right to gain access and participate in education, as well as to benefit from gender-sensitive and gender-responsive educational environments and to obtain meaningful education outcomes that ensure that education benefits translate into greater participation in social, economic and political development of their societies. Achieving gender parity is therefore understood as only a first step towards gender equality. (2012: 21)

Feminism or Gender Equality in Education: GAPs in Access or Achievement

With the incorporation of some feminist views into neoliberal discourses, these contribute to notions of gender parity or gender equality, largely concerned with gender binaries: about girls versus boys and access to and participation within forms of education, focusing on educational achievement. Indeed, an overwhelming emphasis in the political literature, drawing on the social-scientific or research evidence, is now focused on achievement *gaps*.

These are what UNESCO calls the gender parity index (GPI), which can be either positive or negative. The gaps are about the relations between girls and boys and are usually linked to girls' achievements at school, and in access to university. On occasion, this may be seen in association with social class, race and/ or ethnicity, and/or disabilities, but this is often to disparage the progressive feminist arguments, and to insinuate that women's equality has been achieved at the expense of men, working-class men especially.

These ideas about diversity and difference have influenced much social, educational and feminist research over the last thirty years and, as their importance has increased, they have also been used in a range of disparate ways in the political sphere: as either evidence-based policy or policy-based evidence.

A most intriguing example of this is presented by Lord David Willetts, Conservative Minister of State for Universities and Science in the British Coalition Government (2010–14). In his book *The Pinch* (2011), he contributed to what is called 'the feminization crisis'. He argued that working-class men should be favoured over middle-class women in accessing HE, given his fear that 'feminism had trumped egalitarianism' (2011: 208).

Additionally, he provided a similar argument in his appraisal of the changes in HE over the last fifty years. He produced a pamphlet for the fiftieth anniversary of the UK Robbins Report on *Higher Education* (1963) (Willetts 2013). Here, he argued that 'in 2011–2012 . . . 54 per cent of full-time students at UK HEIs were female' (Willetts 2013: 26), arguing that this comes from 'a shift in the gender balance in higher education'.

Willetts added that 'the situation we face in today's society is one that might have seemed unlikely in 1960s Britain, with more women entering university than there are men even submitting a UCAS form. This is a remarkable achievement for women, who were outnumbered in universities by men as recently as the 1990s. *It is also the culmination of a longstanding educational trend, with boys and men finding it harder to overcome obstacles in the way of learning. It is a real challenge for different policy-makers*' (Willetts 2013: 27–8; my emphasis). Willetts clearly laments this shift in the gender balance, not only in higher education (HE) but also in the wider society.

In the US, there are also numerous debates about gender equity in education, dating back over fifty years to the development of women's equality from the Civil Rights Act 1964 and Economic Opportunity Act of 1964, and its subsequent development into the Elementary and Secondary Education Act 1965. A key feature was the amending of the Civil Rights Act 1964 with Title IX specifically on education and discrimination against women from 1972.

While gender equality overall is now on the American agenda, questions of gender-related violence (GRV) and sexual abuse or harassment remain to be addressed, including on university campuses. Nevertheless, President Obama set up a commission to investigate campus sexual assaults in January 2014 (Obama 2014).

In the last two years evidence of campus 'rape cultures' has been emerging in public.

Replacing Hillary Clinton in January 2013, the new Secretary of State in the US, John Kerry, in his first article for a British newspaper (2013: 14), entitled 'Malala's Vital Lesson for US Foreign Policy', stated: 'This is why the United States believes *gender equality* is critical to our shared goals of prosperity, and peace, and investing in women and girls worldwide is critical to advancing US foreign policy' (my emphasis). Thus, he clearly asserted an economic and international competitive argument for gender equality.

However, at a statistical level, the trends that have been noted by Willetts for the UK have also been achieved in the US. *The Chronicle of Higher Education* published its special issue (2 November 2012, part B) with the editor noting: 'It's well known, for example, that female undergraduates outnumber their male counterparts . . . the undergraduate gender gap is especially striking among black students . . . women are advancing in the professoriate as well' (Carolyn Mooney, senior editor, special sections, B3, 2012).

Nevertheless, across all countries of the global North, the question of differential participation in subjects or disciplines remains, with higher concentration of females in the arts, humanities and social sciences, and of males in the more prestigious STEM (science, technology, engineering and maths or medicine) subjects.

Surface Reality of Change across the Globe towards Gender Equality

What is the contemporary situation as regards the 'numbers' of women and men or girls and boys participating in education? How do the figures relate to questions of equality? Of course, this is a complex question because in the majority of countries of the global North schooling for children and young people is compulsory, but what and how they are taught may differ. In addition, sociocultural factors may influence forms of teaching and/or pedagogy as well as the curriculum, and the organization of schools for boys and girls. As regards higher or tertiary education, there remains diversity even in the global North.

UNESCO's (2012) *World Atlas* covered students across forms of schooling, up to and including researchers, but it included very little on the academic or education labour market or forms of employment, whether academic or not. Most interestingly, it is now committed to global gender equality across and including all levels of education. As the authors of the Atlas are social scientists, their arguments touch upon the questions of socio-cultural differences.

The authors argued that the origins of this commitment to equality in education, including for gender, were set in the Millennium Development Goals (MDGs) of 2000, to be achieved by 2015. Unfortunately, this has not been the case. It may be because of the obstacles that they mention, or wider socio-cultural questions. This issue is clearly still a pressing socio-political question, when issues of VAWG are on the global political agenda. The Atlas nevertheless provides the most challenging information about gender equality across the life course (but including also what is called, in this publication, tertiary education: this covers all post-school or post-compulsory education, namely HE and universities).

It also signals how gender equality in education is on the global public agenda in ways in which it was not at the beginning of the twenty-first century, and certainly not as an international issue during the twentieth century. The production of this 'evidence' is an important indicator of public-policy debates about gender equality, including the socio-economic interests of the global powers, as Kerry's (2013) argument illustrates.

The Director-General of UNESCO, Irina Bokova, argued:

> Good policy is sharp policy. It is policy that targets specific problems and bottlenecks. For this, we need a clear picture of what is happening and good data. This first [atlas] . . . responds to this need on one of the most important questions for human rights and sustainable development today. Girls and women remain deprived of full and equal

opportunities for education. *There has been progress towards parity at the primary level, but this tapers off at the secondary level in developing regions. The global economic crisis is deepening inequalities, made worse by cuts in education budgets and stagnating development support.* (UNESCO 2012: foreword; my emphasis)

Gender equality in education has been accepted as a global human right, but how is this interpreted? The term 'gender' is understood as a binary between boys and girls, about educational access and achievements, regardless of the specifics of the curriculum or social and sexual relations within and between teachers and students. The social construction of or nuances in gender or sexual categories are not discussed. There is also only a limited discussion of cultural and social differences in definitions of women and/ or gender and there is no discussion of the social construction of gender or sexuality.

The Atlas concentrates on providing a global overview of both the growth in educational opportunities and their gender specificities. While there is little space for more than broad headlines, some attention is given to economic, geographical and regional differences, including between the 'global North' and the 'global South', and to the changing picture in relation to women's increasing involvement in education across the life-course.

By way of general summary, it is argued that:

The Atlas tells the story of enormous growth in educational opportunities and literacy levels throughout the world over the last four decades . . . During this period the capacity of the world's educational systems more than doubled – from 647 million students in 1970 to 1,397 million in 2009. Enrolments increased from 418 to 702 million pupils at the primary level, from 196 to 531 million at the secondary level, and from 33 to 164 million in higher education . . . The Atlas pays special attention to the issue of gender equality. While educational opportunity expanded over the last four decades for both sexes [*sic*], the gains were particularly striking among girls in terms of access, retention and progression from primary to secondary and beyond. The maps and tables describe patterns of gender parity at all levels of education – pre-primary, primary, secondary and tertiary – and show how these patterns are shaped by factors such as national wealth, geographic location and field of study.

An important theme is that although girls are still disadvantaged in terms of access to education in many countries and regions, they tend to persist and perform at higher rates than boys once they do make it into the education system. Another theme is that all countries face gender equality issues of some sort, including situations where boys are disadvantaged in one way or another. (UNESCO 2012: 9; my emphasis)

This is somewhat similar to the approach taken by Willetts (2013) regarding the changing gender balance.

The authors of the Atlas, as social scientists, argue that there are *four factors* that underlie and shape educational policies and practices in all countries. All of these refer to the changing political and economic balances, and how state policies relate to economic contexts, including the demand for education. They argue that: 'These [four] factors are the impact of population growth on the demand for education, the relationship between levels of national wealth and investment in education, the extent to which national governments are committed to their state education systems, and how such commitment takes on a legal basis in the form of compulsory education policies' (2012: 9).

They show the extent to which education has become compulsory in the majority of countries of the world, with a relatively small number now – four countries – having no compulsory education at all. Nevertheless, the extent of compulsion still varies between the global North and South. They assert that:

The concept of education as a basic right has long been affirmed in most developed countries and has been extended to developing countries as well. An important signal of countries' commitment to the right to education is the number of years for which education is compulsory. The largest number of countries (105) are in the range of 10 to 14 years, while 67 make education compulsory for 7 to 9 years. (p. 18)

They argue that:

> Discussions about gender equity have traditionally focused on finding ways to help girls catch up with boys in terms of access, completion and long-term educational attainment. By such measures boys globally continue to enjoy significant advantages throughout the developing world. This is why both Education for All goals, as well as the MDGs, have put so much emphasis and invested so many resources over the last two decades in 'gender equity' – *meaning helping girls catch up with boys*. (p. 21; my emphasis)

Despite this overly statistical approach and the use of the GPI as opposed to the equality index to measure access, the authors present a rather sophisticated approach to understanding the shifts and changes:

> Many factors have contributed to the increase in women's participation in education, including the fact that higher levels of education and training are becoming necessary to ensure social mobility and to earn higher incomes. The global diffusion of ideas regarding gender equality has also been an important factor, especially in developing countries. But the situation has become increasingly nuanced. Developed countries now talk about gender gaps that favour females in education, and similar patterns are evident at some levels in developing countries even though boys continue to enjoy an advantage in many such countries. This growth reflects changing values and attitudes related to the role and aspirations of women in society. (p. 21)

But then they use rather traditional and somewhat sexist arguments to allay fears about gender equality. They say that 'Also relevant is the fact that stable social processes that make demands on men's masculinity, such as serving as soldiers or demands for labour calling for physical strength, for example construction or mining work, prevent men from participating in the tertiary education system, as they will have other alternatives.'

The Girl or Boy Problem?

In addressing the constraints to gender equality in the global South, however, the authors of the Atlas demonstrate a more nuanced and sophisticated argument about the socio-cultural factors or obstacles, ranging from family and domestic responsibilities to an acknowledgement about cultural factors that may produce sexual harassment and violence, as well as broader political and economic factors. What is clearly buried within a surfeit of statistics about the gender parity index (GPI) is a clear acknowledgement of the silencing of cultural gender norms that maintain gender inequalities. To quote from the report:

> Despite the continued existence of what is sometimes called the 'boy problem' in some countries, the rights of girls to education continues to be inhibited in many developing countries in important respects.
>
> 1. *Constraints with families.* In many countries girls take on domestic responsibilities, including the care of younger siblings, and, depending on the country and the culture, boys often receive preferences when choices have to be made regarding education. For example, in most African countries, such as Kenya, girls may experience domestic work overload, which reduces their interest in pursuing education. Since it is commonly expected that girls should be married off at an early age, parents consider educating their daughters a waste of time and money. The girls are aware of their parents' perceptions regarding their education. They do not find it necessary to work hard because they assume that they will probably drop out of school early.
> 2. *Constraints within society.* These include pressure for early marriage, sexual harassment and violence in and out of educational settings, religious constraints and vulnerability to HIV and AIDS.
> 3. *Policies of school system and educational practices.* School systems in countries of all kinds are not always empowering for girls, nor are they sensitive to their needs through curricula, guidance and counseling services, teaching methods and the presence of appropriate female role models.

4. *Benefits of education.* Even when girls achieve parity in access to
education or academic performance, this parity does not always
lead to equal benefits of education, especially in the job market of
developed countries.

    In short, gender disparities and inequalities are prevalent within
the schooling process in both rich and poor countries. Virtually all
countries must address the gender disparities and inequalities that
shape the ways in which boys and girls progress through the education system. (2012: 25)

They argue about girls' and boys' progress through the education system up to tertiary education. For instance, they point
out that in the global South the rate of children remaining out of
school has fallen by almost 50 per cent.

Despite the substantial number of children who remain out of school,
the proportion is actually declining even though the overall school-age
populations continue to increase. . . the rates of out-of-school children
were relatively stable between 1999 and 2009 for most regions and
declined dramatically in the three areas where the problem had been
most severe: South and West Asia, Arab States, and sub-Saharan Africa.
Progress was greatest in sub-Saharan Africa, where, despite a number
of countries with large out-of-school populations, the overall rate fell
from 41 to 23 percent. (p. 54)

They also show the progress that girls are making relative to boys
in academic subjects, particularly for reading and mathematics, in
developing countries. They state that:

[I]n 2000, girls performed better than boys in a majority of countries
in reading, while boys did better than girls in a majority of countries
in mathematics. Comparable data for 2007 is remarkable in that the
sets of countries in which boys outperformed girls and vice versa were
virtually the same as in 2000. So, too, were the magnitudes of the differences. Abundant evidence exists in countries around the world of
significant gender differences in learning achievement. Specifically,
girls tend to have an advantage in reading achievement compared to

boys, while boys have historically held an advantage in mathematics and science. In many countries girls have been narrowing the gaps in these areas of study, but recent evidence . . . suggests that these gender differences are persisting. (p. 106)

However, they reinforce the arguments made about socio-cultural factors impeding girls' educational progress:

The extent to which girls are disproportionately excluded from education is higher at the secondary level than in primary education and increases further from the lower to the upper secondary levels. There may be various reasons for this: *Emotional and physical dangers may increase as girls grow into young women and face sexual harassment and assault and social demands to conform to traditional gender roles. Lack of bathrooms and other sanitary facilities can be a problem, and the daily journey to school can be unsafe for girls and young women in communities around the world. Traditional conceptions of appropriate roles for both women and men are often pronounced in the technical and vocational aspects of secondary education.* (p. 58; my emphasis).

While barely acknowledging the relatively hidden issues of sexual abuse and harassment to concentrate on what might be considered more palatable arguments about 'access', they do mention socio-cultural factors within schools and educational practices.

Despite the substantial gains that have been made in recent years, access is the single most important cause of disparities against girls in the pursuit of primary and secondary education. But girls also face in-school disadvantages in forms that include biased treatment, harassment and sexist stereotypes in educational content. Boys are less likely than girls to be excluded from education based on their gender, but they also face in-school issues that contribute to higher repetition and dropout rates. (p. 98)

With respect to school-based and compulsory education they therefore conclude that:

Gender disparities can take many different forms across countries. Thus countries need a range of different policies to address the specific inequalities related to school intake, classroom practices and the transition to higher levels of education. Just as most countries take steps to ensure that girls have access to school, they also need policies to address the different disadvantages facing boys and girls that arise at different levels of schooling. (p. 98)

Globalization Has Led to More Attention to Gender Egalitarianism

These changing balances are also carefully elaborated, and presented in tables and maps, with evidence about how the rise in female enrolments has been more rapid in countries of Africa and Asia, given the lower base on which to develop. Moreover, some countries of the 'global North' may be said to have reached saturation and are unable to include more students. In drawing together an overarching conclusion for their Atlas, the authors conclude:

> Female enrolments have increased faster than those for males at all levels, most dramatically in tertiary education . . . Whereas the challenge of gender equality was once seen as a simple matter of increasing female enrolments, the situation is now more nuanced, and every country, developed and developing alike, faces policy issues relating to gender equality.
>
> Girls continue to face discrimination in access to primary education in some countries, and the female edge in tertiary enrolment up through the master's level disappears when it comes to PhDs and careers in research. On the other hand, once girls gain access to education their levels of persistence and attainment often surpass those of males. High repetition and dropout rates among males are significant problems. (2012: 107)

The argument is that there are significant differences between men and women in their approaches to educational achievement and learning, with an emphasis on *girls' resilience through persistence and hard work* (my emphasis), whereas men tend to have a lower threshold of persistence and dropout. However, it is also argued that the external environment, rather than policy prescriptions per se, accounts for women's dramatic increase in involvement. Factors such as poverty and ambition to better themselves encourage women's participation. 'Even though HE leads to individual returns in the form of higher income, women often need to have more education than men to get the same jobs. *Globalization has led to more attention to gender egalitarianism.* Finally, once women gain access to HE they frequently exceed men in grades, evaluations and degree completion' (p. 84; my emphasis).

They also conclude that, while there has been an enormous increase in educational participation within and through HE and beyond, this has not been matched by greater participation in the labour market, especially not in academic or leadership terms. This is, then, one of the key paradoxes of gender equality in education: is it an indication of continuing forms of misogyny, sexism or patriarchal relations in the wider society?

> It must also be noted that over-representation of women in HE has yet to translate into proportional representation in the labour market, especially in leadership and decision-making positions. Even though many women have started to benefit from their countries' improved education systems, they face barriers to the same work opportunities available to men. Women continue to confront discrimination in jobs, disparities in power, voice and political representation and the laws that are prejudicial on the basis of their gender. As a result, well-educated women often end up in jobs where they do not use their full potential and skills. (p. 84)

> [W]omen have reached parity with men in earning bachelor's degrees. They have an edge over men of 56 to 44 percent in master's degrees, but this ratio is exactly reversed at the PhD level. Women receive more bachelor's degrees than men in three of the five regions and more master's degrees in two. *When it comes to PhDs, however, men have the advantage in all regions* . . .

> Despite the narrowing of the gender gap in tertiary enrolment, significant differences are observed in the fields in which men and women

choose to earn degrees . . . The major regional exception to these patterns is Central Asia, which strongly favours women in science and
where female graduates are a minority in the social sciences, business
and law. (pp. 80–1; my emphasis)

The fact remains that men predominate in jobs after the PhD
and especially in relation to research posts. It is only the arts and
social sciences that are dominated by women, including education:
'Among the four fields presented, *education is the most popular with
women.* Women are more likely than men to graduate in this field
in 77 of the 84 countries with data. They account for more than
nine in ten graduates in several countries' (p. 82; my emphasis).
The final argument presented in the Atlas is that:

Despite these achievements however, most of the developing regions
still fall behind on several aspects of gender equality. It is often the
case where a better level of education doesn't necessarily translate into
better employment opportunities. Even though women outperform
men in education, they still face significant shortfalls and discrimination in the labour market and end up in jobs where they don't use
any of their skills. However, even though education is not the only
input into women's empowerment it is nonetheless a central one.
(p. 107)

Conclusions

It is quite clear that there is a complexity of arguments about
gender equality in education at both the national and international
levels. While, if we only take a statistical approach, it may appear
that gender equality in education has been achieved, this does
not take account of the structural and normative contexts. Many
feminists do not accept these rather simplistic statistical arguments
and address the question about how to go beyond the simple
numbers game. Indeed, Louise Morley (2013) argues that these
are 'misogyny masquerading as metrics'. She argues for changing

the 'rules of the game' whereby male power remains embedded within the structures of leadership and organization. She is one of the feminists arguing for more sophisticated approaches to gender, women and education.

3

Feminist Political Campaigns on Gender and Violence

Introduction

I now look at how feminists have campaigned for socio-political changes in the legal position of women and girls over the last few centuries, emphasizing the twenty-first century. We have already seen how notions of both feminism and gender equality are incorporated into neoliberal global agendas. Here, I focus on the changing international context, and the specificities of each of the countries that we worked with for the GAP project across the EU: the UK and Ireland (as examples of anglophone traditions), and Italy and Spain (as examples of Latin countries). I also consider briefly other countries of the 'global North', especially the US, and the links across the UN. I focus on women's achievements with respect to legislation for women's rights, gender equality and gender-related violence (GRV).

There has been a secular trend towards transforming women's 'political' lives and international women's rights over the last 150 years. Women's rights campaigners and the shifting political economy have contributed to the changing balance between notions of state responsibility for social welfare, women and children especially, and the role of civil society. The relations between individual and collective responsibilities, while always shifting, have moved inexorably towards a less interventionist state, in the twenty-first century, despite the growth of academic capitalism. Recently, this has been more to do with enhancing economic competitiveness than with transforming women's lives. But legislation creates conditions of possibility in our everyday lives and in relation with the struggle against GRV.

Early feminist campaigns revolved around women's suffrage, which became a very hard-fought and, at times, violent process. These related to women's responsibilities as wives, mothers and carers, and associated questions of children's rights and responsibilities. Linked to these have been highly contentious debates about sexual abuse and domestic or family violence, leading eventually to notions of GRV.

All the various countries have slightly different cultures and traditions, especially around religion and the politics of transforming women's lives. Feminist campaigns have taken different forms because of these socio-cultural differences, especially in relation to religion and traditional 'gender norms'. There are particular national differences with, for instance, civil society in Spain recognizing GRV legislation. Campaigns around women's rights, followed by gender equality and GRV, have not proceeded in parallel, but rather in response to specific changing circumstances and/or events.

The reason that we, on the GAP project, developed an analysis of the legislation relevant to gender equality and GRV was because we found that youth professionals' abilities to navigate the legislative waters have often been limited by lack of knowledge and understanding of relevant pieces of legislation and their practical applications. We were aware from our previous studies (Alldred and David 2007; Biglia and Velazco 2012) that there were no core curricula about women's rights; nor about women's history or equality in compulsory education, and not necessarily in professional training courses.

An aim of the project was therefore to analyse the relevant legal frameworks and political discourses of the participating countries and their relation to EU legislation. We produced an account of the evolution of the EU's supranational powers and how these relate to each national context. It also describes current legislation on GRV, including gender and sex discrimination (Alldred and David 2015: 17; Alldred and Biglia 2015; Biglia, Olivella and Cagliero 2015).

Stages of Development of Gender-Equality Policies: 1945–2015

We argue that there have been at least four 'stages' in the development of gender-equality policies, linked with GRV, in the postwar period, from 1945. Prior to that, 'first-wave feminists' in the global North had successfully campaigned for political suffrage, although in some places this was a slow process across the first half of the twentieth century.

First, with the setting up of the UN, the postwar period up to the 1960s–70s was marked by progressive and social democratic or at least socially liberal policies, across the global North. There was a tacit commitment to the idea of women's rights being part of human or civil rights, although endorsement within the political system was not strong. It was also a period of relative quiescence as regards feminist activism.

During the 1960s and 1970s, across Europe and North America – the global North – feminists began to stir through the Women's Liberation Movement (WLM), slowly becoming known as second-wave feminism. Their campaigns were linked, as we have seen, with civil and social rights movements, on a platform for women's rights and socio-economic equality with men.

Second, the process of change in the EU has paralleled that of the UN, moving from women's equality to more nuanced questions. EU legal interventions on gender violence have evolved over time as, progressively, EU international treaties have moved the Union's powers from the economic sphere to the social.

Originally, in the 1950s and 1960s, the European Economic Community (EEC) focused upon economic objectives for gender equalities. Article 119 of the 1957 Treaty of Rome specifically addressed wage parity between men and women. In the 1980s, as the direct result of campaigning by women's groups, the EU developed *applied* measures (through Directive 76/207/EEC), and equal opportunities programmes and a board to introduce positive action were created (Vara and Carrasco 2003).

There was an uneven process across countries of the EU as many only began to join during the 1970s and 1980s, marking their legal convergence with European standards. While Italy was a founding member with France and Germany in the early 1950s, the UK and Ireland joined the EU in 1973, and Spain in 1986. During the 1970s, countries both resisted and implemented legislation on equal opportunities and issues of sex discrimination. EU and Italian policies institutionalized some aspects of the feminist movement.

Paradoxically, just as second-wave feminists were beginning to find their voice in the political arena with 'demands on the state' for changing policies around equal [educational] opportunities, inter alia, there was a conservative political backlash against feminist demands from the 1980s onwards. This second stage was marked by a conservative turn, in the UK and in the US especially. Other countries of the EU tended to be more ambivalent about the processes.

Margaret Thatcher was the first woman to be appointed as British prime minister (1979–90), representing a turn away from social liberalism and democracy (David 2003). While she was fiscally conservative, she was not totally opposed to changing women's rights. Indeed, under her administration some women's opportunities in education and employment were opened up, while others were closed down, particularly for single- or lone-parent families. This was similar to the situation in the US, while Ronald Reagan was president. There were both gains and losses for women's rights and equality across the countries of the EU and indeed the UN.

However, by the early 1990s, the growth of 'global feminism' had led to more general political acceptance of some demands for social legislation, despite growing fiscal conservatism. This stage can be characterized by the move towards gender mainstreaming across the EU policies and in other countries of the global North, during the 1990s. Nevertheless, there was strong resistance to gender mainstreaming from conservative governments in the US, the UK, Spain and Italy.

On the other hand, the progressive government in Ireland introduced legal improvements around gender mainstreaming. The expansion of the EU in the 1990s to include countries that championed gender issues, such as Austria, Finland and Sweden, also resulted in a more gender-sensitive approach to EU policymaking (Hafner-Burton and Pollock 2000). It was not until the 1997 Treaty of Amsterdam that the EU acquired the power actively to intervene in relation to workplace sex/gender discrimination.

Later, gender mainstreaming, as a policy notion, became more commonplace in the early twenty-first century across the EU, in response to growing economic and social demands for women's involvement in employment and politics. This stage is characterized by the implementation of gender mainstreaming as policy in progressive governments across the EU.

The institutionalization of some feminisms and the mainstreaming of their demands (Walby 2002) effected changes in political rhetoric. Among other things, they led to greater attention being paid to the use of sexist and homophobic language (Millns and Skeet 2013), and they were useful when it came to developing certain gender policies. However, the institutionalization also brought about a co-optation of many feminist claims (Montoya 2009). This is well illustrated by the mainstreaming of the term 'gender'.

On the one hand, the use of the concept made it possible to recognize the socio-cultural norms and values, pressures and incentives involved in constructing gendered subjects and a binary, heterosexual order. On the other hand, the term is frequently used to dismiss the necessity of feminist analyses. In fact, it is mostly employed in mainstreaming policies that tend not to be sensitive to central feminist issues in regard to power, hierarchies and difference (Biglia and Olivella-Quintana 2014).

By the second decade of the twenty-first century, the political tendency of most governments across the EU and the global North became that of 'austerity', linked with the global economic crisis, the security paradigm and the rise of conservative parties in Europe. With the 2007 Treaty of Lisbon, there was a further expansion of EU powers to include 'security' in its broadest sense. This involved the inclusion of security in policymaking and several EU directives that addressed GRV through a security lens, such as Directive 2011/92/EU of the European Parliament and of the Council of 13 December 2011, on combating the sexual abuse and sexual exploitation of children and child pornography (Alldred and David 2015: 18).

The inclusion of gender (but not GRV) as a specific focus of EU policymaking meant that tackling gender inequality became one of its most important social objectives. But achieving gender equality through the EU is problematic as it has limited powers and many are met through the implementation of 'soft' policies, which do not have the legal status of directives but still impact on member states. It remains for individual states to interpret and implement them (Alldred and David 2015: 23).

The treaties are binding agreements between EU member countries and are the basic documents whose goals are achieved by regulations and decisions (that are binding), directives (that set out goals to be achieved), recommendations and opinions: therefore there are conceptual tensions. In fact, the terminology used in national laws is frequently contradictory, with different expressions for the same forms of violence and the same expression for different forms of violence.

We note that the shift from labour discrimination to risk/security framing of GRV by the EU goes hand-in-hand with the design of national penal GRV legislation which does not include preventative or educational measures in most partner countries, considering GRV as a private rather than a social responsibility. More specifically, GRV is mainly seen as about male perpetrators in adult heterosexual relations. Furthermore, the frequent use of gender-neutral language in laws produces inattention to gendered power relations.

I turn now to a brief outline of the richness and diversity of these campaigns. Why is it that a commitment to gender equality has not been sufficient to enable tackling questions of GRV or domestic and sexual abuse, including child sexual abuse?

Evidence about First-Wave Feminist Campaigns

During the first half of the twentieth century, there were many diverse campaigns for transformations in women's lives, across the global North. In addition to campaigns for women's suffrage, there were campaigns about the extent and fairness of women's education, women's employment and property rights, and demands for changes in attitudes towards women's sexual health, especially in relation to children.

A host of writers began to develop the evidence on which to base campaigns. Of particular note were the Swedish couple Gunnar and Alva Myrdal, who began the process of arguing for support for families, women in particular, during the 1920s. Alva was a sociologist, and her husband an economist. It was their involvement in writing about families and race relations, in the US, that sealed their international reputation as social democrats. After the end of the Second World War, they amongst others became actively involved in developing the UN as a major peace-keeping organization. Wikipedia (2016b) notes:

> [I]n the late 1940s [Alva] became involved in international issues with the UN, appointed to head its section on welfare policy in 1949, while her husband had become Executive Secretary of the UN Economic Commission for Europe in 1947. From 1950 to 1955, she was chairman of UNESCO's social science section – the first woman to hold such prominent positions in the UN [. . .] A vocal supporter of disarmament, Myrdal received the Nobel Peace Prize in 1982.

Her husband, Gunnar Myrdal had received the Nobel Prize for Economics in 1974. They demonstrate the internationalization of these diverse campaigns for women's rights, including the involvement of the UN.

Similarly, Simone de Beauvoir and Jean-Paul Sartre illustrate, as an intellectual and more radical couple in France, the extent to which broader issues were developing in the middle of the twentieth century, and particularly as a result of the ending of the Second World War. De Beauvoir's study *The Second Sex* – an original account of women's subordination – was published to critical acclaim in 1949 in France and 1953 in Britain. Hers was an influential text that contributed to the rise of second-wave feminism. But many of the developments in the more nuanced arguments for women's equality only began to develop in the later postwar period.

Olive Banks (1986), the renowned British feminist sociologist of education, identified British first-wave feminists in terms of their social and educational origins and their campaigns. She focused upon the UK but did not distinguish between the four countries, although Scotland and Northern Ireland have clear differences from England and Wales. Interestingly, we found in the GAP work project that Scotland is the only country in the UK that recognizes a gender-based definition of domestic abuse (Lombardo and Bustelo 2012).

Banks (1986) developed a cohort analysis of first-wave feminists: 'the data on which this study is based, therefore, is mainly biographical in nature although the method of analysis is primarily sociological . . . Feminism like socialism is in many ways impossible to define in any really objective way so that, in the last resort, the choice . . . is, and must be, a very personal one' (Banks 1986: 2).

She showed first how her 'best-known' feminists tended to be middle class and concentrate on political campaigning largely around questions of women's participation in socio-political movements. These campaigns, while around women's subordinate positions, differed according to contexts. They were often also linked with educational and social concerns, and on occasion linked with questions of poverty and family responsibilities, as well as women's rights to work and independence from patriarchal authority.

Banks argued that:

One of the most striking findings of the study . . . is the extent to which 'first wave' feminism not only changed the nature of its political affiliations at some time towards the end of the nineteenth century, but in doing so changed, in a fairly dramatic way, the whole nature of feminism itself . . . By the beginning of the twentieth century the nineteenth-century dominance of the equal rights tradition had been largely replaced by socialist feminism . . . Thus differences in religious and particularly in political affiliation can be demonstrated to be related both to feminist involvement in particular campaigns and . . . to aspects of feminist ideology. (Banks 1986: 6–8)

Simon Szreter, the educational historian, in an obituary of Banks, argued that she 'demonstrated that Victorian feminism was composed of many strands and that there were continuities between "first" and "second wave". It is her achievement that both of these are now commonplaces of historical knowledge' (Szreter 2006). What Szreter calls 'commonplaces of historical knowledge' are now 'received wisdom' or the 'feminist canon' (Davis and Evans 2011). Yet these are more complex than Szreter acknowledges.

The questions of the relations between first-, second- and indeed third-wave feminism and beyond is also in dispute as Banks herself, like many other feminists born in the first three decades of the twentieth century (such as de Beauvoir, Friedan, Myrdal), does not fall easily into the waves or generations as Banks defined them, in terms of their birth dates. It was indeed their education, writings and dates of publication that were the more important, with both de Beauvoir (born 1908 in France) and Friedan (born 1921 in Peoria, US) being seen as foundational to second-wave feminism although not born in that generation, and Banks (born 1923 in England) together with Alva Myrdal (born 1902), the Swedish sociologist, foundational to feminist sociology.

Nevertheless, Banks also asserted that:

All the variations within feminism . . . however they are labelled, have in common a sense of dissatisfaction with the condition of women's lives and opportunities, coupled with a belief that women's disabilities arise not from nature itself, nor indeed from any of the ills which afflict humankind as such, but from the way in which women's desires and abilities have been made subordinate to the needs, desires, and interests of men. This subordination of women is reflected in law, custom, and

also in much of religion . . . Within this very broad definition of feminism there is room for a great variety of opinions on the nature and
extent of the changes that might be needed to end the subordination
of women to men. It also allows for different theories of the cause of
women's subordination, and different strategies for bringing it to an
end, as well as different views on the relationship between sex and
gender. Feminism therefore involves not only a critique of women's
subordination but a belief, or perhaps a faith, that it is possible to
bring it to an end. For this reason it consists of both an ideology and a
programme of action. (Banks 1986: 164)

Few of the first-wave feminist campaigns were publicly associated with questions of sex, sexual health and sexual abuse, although
Josephine Butler, an evangelical Christian, married to the head-
master of Liverpool College, campaigned in the 1850s and 1860s
about the sexual diseases that women, including married women,
tended to contract in association with men linked to the armed
forces. Indeed, her campaigns against the Contagious Diseases Acts
were successful resulting in their repeal in 1886; Grant 2016: 19) in
the 1860s. However, feminists tended to separate their campaigns
from her, especially around women's education, to prevent con-
tamination by association (David 2015a).

Moreover, the definitions of acceptable sexual activity tended at
that time to be more circumscribed for men as well as for women.
Penetrative homosexual male practices were punishable by death
until 1861 and, later, by prison (Brady 2005). Intriguingly, it was
this kind of legislation that the well-known French philosopher
Michel Foucault concentrated on analysing, in his early studies
of the power of the state. He also initiated studies of the role of
discipline and control through such informal regulatory methods
(Foucault 1973). Many second- to third-wave feminists have
adopted Foucault's theoretical approach, in a movement that
became known as post-structuralism.

Industrialization and colonial expansion in the nineteenth
century forced processes of social change and eventual legislation
around women's property rights and rights to education. The
women's educational movement was one of the first to campaign

successfully for both elementary and secondary education, and also some modicum of higher education for women, although it was different from the provisions for men. These differences in types of provision continued until well into the twentieth century, including around 'the differentiation of the curriculum for the sexes' (David 2015a; Biglia and Velasco 2012). This was the case internationally as well as in the UK. The processes of change in the US, for example, occurred earlier than in the UK.

Campaigns for Women's Suffrage

British women campaigners for political rights were either suffragettes or suffragists, and the distinctions between the two were over the extent to which they questioned the status quo and the patriarchal social order, in terms of acquiescing to the cultural and sexual norms of the time (David 2015a). Suffragists were willing to accept the socio-political order, whereas suffragettes took direct action in contesting the laws of the time. In the UK, the first-wave feminist National Union of Women's Suffrage Societies (NUWSS) was formed in 1897 and the National Union of Societies for Women's Citizenship (NUSEC) was formed a year later (Grant 2016).

The term 'suffragette' was particularly associated with activists in the British Women's Social and Political Union (WSPU), formed in 1903 and led by the Pankhursts, who were influenced by Russian methods of protest such as hunger strikes. Other tactics employed by members included chaining themselves to railings to provoke an arrest, pouring harsh chemicals into mailboxes, breaking windows at prestige buildings, and night-time arson at unoccupied buildings. Indeed, many were imprisoned for what were seen as illegal actions, and many took the view that they should further resist by refusal to eat. This led to many of them being force-fed and suffering grave health complications.

There were many contests within and between the various British suffrage groups, over direct action and individual or collective and socialist methods. Their campaigning took place over at least a twenty- to thirty-year period, from the 1890s into the twentieth century, when suffrage was eventually granted. Similar feminist campaigns were also waged in other countries and contexts, although the timescales tended to differ. Other European countries, Italy and Spain, for example, did not have such political campaigns. British activists followed in the footsteps of those in the US and, intriguingly, New Zealand.

US Women's Rights Campaigners

Early women's rights campaigners in the US met at Seneca Falls, upstate New York, in 1848. The meeting was advertised as 'a convention to discuss the social, civil, and religious condition and rights of woman'. It was soon followed by other women's rights conventions and a series of annual National Women's Rights Conventions from 1850. There were heated debates about women's suffrage, including men's participation. By 1851, the issue of women's right to vote had become a central tenet of the US women's rights movement. This question of suffrage was included in annual conventions until the outbreak of the American Civil War in 1861.

Yet it was another sixty years before women were afforded the vote in the US, in 1920, when the Nineteenth Amendment to the US Constitution was ratified. The National Women's Party created a celebratory banner of purple for justice, white for purity of intent and gold for courage. The thirty-six stars represent the states that ratified the amendment. Suffrage was extended to women across the US in time for the 1920 presidential election. Of the initial 100 women signatories to the Declaration of Sentiments in 1861, only one was alive by the time of its passing and she was too unwell by then to vote in 1920.

Before that time, in the US, women over the age of twenty-one were allowed to vote in the western territories of Wyoming from 1869, and in Utah from 1870, and in most states outside the South by 1919. Women over twenty-one were allowed to vote in Canada (except Quebec) from 1919.

International Women's Suffrage: 1900–1945

By the early twentieth century, several countries had afforded women the right to vote. Intriguingly, one of the countries of the British Commonwealth was the first to give women the right to vote. New Zealand was the first self-governing country to grant suffrage in 1893, when all women over the age of twenty-one were permitted to vote in parliamentary elections. Women in South Australia achieved the same right and also became the first to obtain the right to stand for Parliament in 1895.

Women in Britain over the age of thirty, meeting certain property qualifications, were given the right to vote in 1918. This was after two decades of campaigning and at the end of the First World War. Ten years later, after more protest, in 1928 suffrage was extended to all British women over the age of twenty-one. Campaigns for women's suffrage and women's right to property were also slower in Ireland, Italy and Spain. Many countries set up International Women's Day (IWD) in March as a symbol of women's campaigns.

The Republic of Ireland, being a Catholic country, banned women from political participation, and only single women were allowed to own property in the nineteenth century (O'Riordan 2011). GRV was widespread but remained silenced (Ryan 2010), while there was deep hostility to homosexuality due to Victorian policies imposed by British colonizers (Conrad 2001). Emergent Irish nationalism and republicanism drew their narratives from tradition and Catholic morality, producing very gendered discourses, and institutional discrimination against women may be identified in such legal documents as the 1937 Irish Constitution (Crowley and Kitchin 2008). Nevertheless, in 1918, partial suffrage was granted to women when Ireland was still part of the UK. Equal suffrage was granted upon independence from the UK in 1922.

As a result of women's suffrage campaigning in Italy, legislation for women's suffrage was achieved in 1922. At the time, curiously, there was a fascist dictatorship (1922–43) and so suffrage was not implemented, with women being relegated to the home (Silvestrini 2007). Abortion and birth control were also forbidden, given that it was a Catholic country. But there were policies around sexual violence and rape, and crimes against public morality and decency. Nevertheless, men retained the legal power to control the movement of wives, and homosexuality was punishable as a public scandal. Finally, in 1945, women were afforded the vote along with the rise of democracy, and so eventually there was official political equality between sexes (Carlassare 2010).

Spain was the last of these European countries, however, to afford women the vote: this was during the First Republic, proclaimed in 1931, replacing the monarchy of Alfonso XIII, where it also become illegal to discriminate for sexual reasons and several laws that empowered women were approved, including the right to divorce, and reproductive rights (Núñez 1998). Nonetheless, Franco's dictatorship (1939–78) imposed serious restrictions regarding sexuality and reproduction; women were imprisoned for abortion, adultery or prostitution (Larumbe 2004), and homosexuality was a crime (Osborne 2006; Alldred and David 2015: 21; Biglia, Olivella and Cagliero 2015).

Stages in Political Recognition of Women's Equality: 1945–95

There was widespread change in approaches to civil, human and women's rights in the postwar era. As we saw in the previous chapter, there were fifty-one member states of the original UN in 1945. Following widespread decolonization in the 1960s, member states had almost quadrupled by 2015. The organization is financed by assessed and voluntary contributions from its member states and, by the 1970s, its budget for economic and social development programmes far outstripped its spending on peacekeeping. These not only included women's rights but also children's rights, which slowly became associated with women's rights over a forty-year period.

Most European countries started to introduce a more democratic approach to women in their legislation in the postwar period. Nonetheless, these changes did not apply simultaneously in all the countries analysed, nor did they apply to the same area. The EU focus on equality in the labour market was followed most closely in the UK. In Italy, many efforts were made for recovering basic rights that had been banned or outlawed during the Fascist regime and, in the 1970s, there was a strong feminist 'street mobilization'. In Ireland, women's rights were sometimes obscured by infighting. And it was not until the late 1970s that changes began to occur in Spain, as the former Spanish dictatorship did not sanction change.

I will briefly consider the period of the 1950s through to the 1990s across the four countries within Europe, and pay some attention to the US, before setting the scene for a more specific consideration of developments in gender equality and GRV over the last two decades.

In the UK, during the war many women were recruited into the labour force to replace the men who were fighting, but afterwards most married women were forced to return home and care for their young children, endorsed by what has become known as Bowlbyism (New and David 1985). This was the theory of the psychologist John Bowlby that children were better cared for at home by their mothers than by others. At the same time, however, the British welfare state was created through the social democracy of the Labour government and was a form of social protection for women and children, as second-wave feminists have argued (Land 1976; Wilson 1977).

Educational opportunities, initially for the middle classes, were extended through the 1944 Education Act, and slowly began to influence girls' opportunities (David 2015a). As the 1950s wore on, women began to return to the labour market and, by the 1960s, feminist campaigns began to bear fruit. For example, the Labour government of 1964–70 was instrumental in beginning a slow process of improvements in gender politics. The 1967 Abortion Act allowed for women's choice, and the Sexual Offences Act 1967 decriminalized 'homosexual acts' in private between adult men.

Second-wave feminist activism around domestic violence usually focused on men's violence against women and so has tended to work with a concept of gender-based violence (GBV). Gay Liberation movements, and certainly in the UK where the GAP project was conceived, were arguably patchy in their problematization of gender and support for women's struggles in the early 1970s, through second-wave feminism (McIntosh 1968). By the end of the 1960s, the Labour government had passed the Equal Pay Act 1970, to be implemented by 1975. But changes towards a more conservative government in the 1970s meant that this legislation was implemented together with the Sex Discrimination Act of 1975. This led to the setting up of an Equal Opportunities Commission (EOC) regarding rights in employment and education, elimination of discrimination and promoting equality of opportunities between men and women (David 2015a).

This legislation occurred at the same time as the UK joined the European Economic Commission (EEC), precursor of the EU (Millns and Skeet 2013). There was a distinct drive to recognize inequality and discrimination underpinning both the Sex Discrimination Act 1975 and the Race Relations Act 1976, and to render unlawful sex discrimination on grounds of marriage (usually affecting married women). However, from the 1970s to the 1990s, successive Conservative governments marginalized feminists, associated with a weak left, and women took up positions of power without feminist sensibilities prevailing (Alldred and David 2015: 22). The struggle over the representation and care demanded by HIV/AIDS from the 1970s to the 1990s is usually viewed as a key mobilizer and, in UK cultural politics, resistance to the Criminal Justice Act (1986) helped undermine a politics based on identity categories in practice, not only in academic studies.

In the US, in the 1960s, developments in anti-discrimination legislation took place, from which the UK and other countries of Europe borrowed. For instance, the Great Society legislation of the 1960s, passed under President Johnson, in the aftermath of Kennedy's assassination in 1963 (the same year that the National Organization of Women (NOW) was launched) led to major changes in the approaches to forms of discrimination, including against women. The Economic Opportunity Act 1964 allowed for the 'accidental' inclusion of women as one of the categories of concern, alongside the Civil Rights Act 1964, which also addressed racial discrimination primarily. Similarly, the Elementary and Secondary Education Act (ESEA) 1965 also raised this question of women's rights in education. And specific forms of sex discrimination in education were included under Title IX from 1972.

As the 1970s wore on, in the US women's rights groups under the NOW, which had been influential in the late 1960s, began to argue for an Equal Rights Amendment (ERA) to the US Constitution. However, this did not achieve the two-thirds majority in the requisite time period and so the amendment was dropped in 1980, in large part due to a very conservative backlash, orchestrated against women's recruitment into the armed forces.

Nevertheless, the UK and the US serve as beacons of second-wave feminist political achievements in comparison with Ireland, Italy and Spain during the second half of the twentieth century. In Ireland, feminist pressure about the entry of Ireland into the EEC in 1973, combined with the economic growth of the 1980s, enabled some subversion of traditional gender roles and opened space for more progressive equality agendas (Equality Authority 2012; Nash 2013). The election of Mary Robinson as the Republic's president in 1990 symbolized the reshaping of the Irish political imagination in the area of gender and sexuality (Meaney 1991), with concepts of violence against women (VAW) and domestic violence appearing for the first time in the political arena (Kearns, Coen and Canavan 2008) and leading to the enactment of the Domestic Violence Act 1996.

In the 1970s in Italy there was a strong flowering of street politics and the women's movement, but the power of the Catholic Church meant that new laws about gender violence and LGBT (lesbian, gay, bisexual, transgender) were not recognized. By 1996, during the Second Republic, the first law against sexual violence was passed, followed slightly later, in 2001, with legislation concerning violence in families (Alldred and David 2015: 19).

The return to liberal democracy in Spain, in 1977, helped the rapid adaptation to European norms such as human rights (Dema 2008), while the implementation of the Constitution included abolition of fascist laws that had criminalized LGTB activity. But conservative governments between 1996 and 2004 introduced regressive policies (Bonet 2007), and a comprehensive law against GRV and various bills to legalize same-sex marriage were rejected, despite a strong feminist movement.

1995 to 2015: A New Wave of Gender Equality in the Twenty-first Century?

The new wave of gender equality in the twenty-first century is beginning to include GRV, within Europe, and especially through the EU, including links with the UK, Ireland, Italy and Spain, and other examples such as the European Institute of Gender Equality. There are no EU directives directly focusing on GRV, but aspects such as the sexual abuse or sexual exploitation of children, fundamental rights and the protection of victims of crime are addressed in conjunction with other non–GRV topics (Alldred and Biglia 2015). In addition, the Council of Europe Convention on preventing and combating violence against women is very relevant. It is a binding agreement offering a comprehensive approach to VAW. However, it is important to note that although Italy, Spain and the UK are signatories, Ireland is not, and the Convention has yet to be enforced in the UK.

More importantly, there are changes because of the UN's developments on the End Violence Against Women coalition (EVAW). Violence against women and girls (VAWG) consists, collectively, of violent acts that are primarily or exclusively committed against women, sometimes considered a hate crime. This type of violence targets a specific group with the victim's gender as a primary motive (GBV), meaning that the acts of violence are committed against women expressly because they are women. Nevertheless, this is not always threaded through British or American legislation.

The UN General Assembly adopted the Declaration on the Elimination of Violence Against Women (DEVAW) in 1993, as we saw. Contained within it is the recognition of 'the urgent need for the universal application to women of the rights and principles with regard to equality, security, liberty, integrity and dignity of all human beings'. The Resolution is often seen as complementary to, and a strengthening of, the work of the Convention on the Elimination of All Forms of Discrimination Against Women (CEDAW). It embodies the same rights and principles as those enshrined in such instruments as the Universal Declaration of Human Rights, and Articles 1 and 2 provide the most widely used definition of VAW.

In addition, three contexts of violence are differentiated: 'family, community and state. Most of the violations, at all three levels, concern women's sexuality, reproductive capacity and their right to decide over their own body. This includes physical, sexual and psychological violence occurring: first, in the family – wife-battering, sexual abuse of female children in the household, dowry-related violence, marital rape, and female genital mutilation and other traditional practices harmful to women, non-spousal violence and violence related to exploitation; second, within the general community – rape, sexual abuse, sexual harassment and intimidation at work and education institutions, trafficking in women and forced prostitution; and, third, perpetrated or condoned by the state, wherever it occurs' (Symonides and Volodin 1999: 53; UN 1993).

The UN DEVAW also states that: 'violence against women is a manifestation of *historically unequal power relations between men and women*' and that 'violence against women is one of the crucial social mechanisms by which women are forced into a subordinate position compared with men' (my emphasis). Wikipedia (2016a) provides an overview:

> The Secretary General of the UN declared in a 2006 report posted on the UNIFEM website that: 'Violence against women and girls is a problem of pandemic proportions. At least one out of every three women around the world has been beaten, coerced into sex, or otherwise abused in her lifetime with the abuser usually someone known to her.'
>
> [. . .] The WHO, in its research on VAW, categorized it as occurring through five stages of the life cycle: (1) pre-birth; (2) infancy; (3) girlhood; (4) adolescence and adulthood; and (5) elderly.

In recent years, there has been a trend of approaching VAWG at an international level, through instruments such as conventions; or, in the EU, through directives, such as the directive against sexual harassment, and the directive against human trafficking.

The powers of the EU are less than twenty years old but the EU has been responsive to feminist and women's rights pressure or activism (Alldred and Biglia 2015). As noted earlier, the EU's Daphne programmes have responded to the need for more research and training on gender equality and associated GRV.

Similarly, in the twenty-first century, the British New Labour governments (1997–2010) made significant improvements in legislation about gender (Thiara 2007) with the Domestic Violence, Crime and Victim Act 2004, the 2009 Violence Against Women group cross-departmental strategy, and LGBT protections under the Equality Act 2010. There was also equalization in 2003 of the age of consent regardless of sexual orientation, recognition of gender reassignment rights and the Marriage Act 2013 that extended the status of marriage to same-sex couples. Nevertheless, no one comprehensive Act addressed GRV, although different acts address GRV themes. Most legislation is gender-neutral and the gendering of violence is generally not considered. For example, the same laws can be used both to protect the privacy of celebrities and against sexual harassment (Callender-Smith 2014).

The paradigm of GRV is therefore an egalitarian one that ignores the effects of patriarchal power relations and hides sexism behind alleged neutrality. GRV as a concept recognizes domestic violence in the home and private sphere as individual acts. But the legislation is inclusive in that it considers violence (in any direction) between members of a family, a household or a partner relation, whether living together or not.

The Domestic Violence Crime and Victims Act 2004 updated protective measures (preventative in the legal sense) of the Family Law Act 1996, such as occupation and non-molestation orders (molestation defined as harassment, not sexually), which young people can apply for against specific other people (including under-eighteens). It brought stronger sanctions, with legal action by the state, not an individual, and gave cohabiting same-sex couples the same options as heterosexual couples, making non-molestation orders available to couples who have not lived together or been married.

The UK Children Act 1989 also offered more protection, and was extended in 2004 when the post of Children's Commissioner was created, concerned with issues like child sex abuse and teenage pregnancy. Reports from the Office of the Children's Commissioner have begun to take on board notions of child abuse generally and child sexual abuse, together with the development of Criminal Records Boards, including official concern about sexual consent.

There is, however, a body of further legislation more focused on rights (instead of offences) that is linguistically less neutral, but, with the exception of the Gender Recognition Act (GRA) 2004 and, in some respects, the Equality Act 2010, most of this legislation does not acknowledge a feminist or gender perspective. Nor does legislation take account of intersectionality, but occasionally a multi-discrimination approach is used. Recent legal moves acknowledge that inequality and discrimination cannot only be recognizable on the basis of someone's identity: the Equality Act 2010 allows not only for being a member of one of the six 'protected characteristics', but for being *perceived or presumed to be* a member of this group. Clearly, this has been a key sticking point in challenging homophobic violence and abuse.

The adult-centred nature of equalities law, especially the Gender Reassignment Act 2004's protection for adults, as those who have undergone gender reassignment, is of limited value in protecting either those undergoing transition or who remain gender non-conforming (arguably, where young people need protection (Alldred and David 2015: 23)). The Sex Offences Act 2003 sought to protect young people, adults and vulnerable people, and so complicates by age, as well as equalizing the age of consent for same-sex activity. It distinguishes 'sex activity with a child' from rape, in the case of thirteen- to sixteen-year-olds where lack of consent is not alleged, but for those of twelve and under, the offence is rape irrespective of a child's expressed wishes.

The fragmented and ungendered form of the legislation was probably one of the reasons for the absence of practical, preventative measures. On the whole, the English legislative framework probably takes LGBT people into greatest consideration, and several laws explicitly recognize same-sex relations for the occurrence of GRV. During 2010–15 the Coalition government's approach to social justice was laissez-faire: hence it ignored human rights legislation and implemented regressive educational policies. Guidance gave health staff responsibility for recognizing and responding to domestic violence (DV) and abuse. From an equalities perspective, this is weak but shapes how British professional and youth practitioners treat GRV (Alldred and David 2015: 23).

In Ireland, following the publication of the 1997 report of the task force on VAWG, the National Steering Committee on VAW was created. Years of LGBT activism led to the decriminalization of same-sex sexual activity in 1993, while the Employment Equality Act 1998 made discrimination based on sexual orientation illegal. Subsequent legislation addressed violence among married and cohabiting couples, FGM, rape and sexual assault, and child sexual abuse. In the Equality Act, institutional gender violence is approached as a form of discrimination, but confusion exists in the language between sex and gender.

There is no comprehensive Irish approach to GRV, but a focus on some manifestations of the problem, within a predominantly penal framework. The most common areas of intervention concern children, health and family policies, conceptualized through a religious and Catholic framing. GRV is therefore a private problem with no emphasis on preventative measures or structural causes. Only individuals (as opposed to entire institutions or boards of governors) can be held accountable or responsible for offences.

Despite anti-discrimination legislation about sexual orientation, the specific GRV needs of young and LGBT people are not addressed in Ireland's legal framework. Youth appears as gender-neutral, being depicted as vulnerable, lacking in agency, and as potential victims of several offences, mostly related to sexuality. The assumption that gender- and age-language neutrality in legislation would allow equal treatment hides a heterosexual and adult-centric approach that tends to dismiss differences. In general, the legislation fails in assuming any kind of intersectional or even multi-layered discrimination approach. In the few cases in which there are institutional mechanisms to safeguard against GRV, these are not supported by any specific measures such as educational interventions (Alldred and David 2015: 20).

In Italy, currently, there is no law solely and directly addressing GRV in its full complexity. Under Berlusconi as president, gender violence was mostly treated as a problem of public order and as a public safety issue, and there were concerns about gender equality in the workplace. When GRV legislation was passed it was often in response to high-profile cases of sexual violence perpetrated by foreign nationals. Legal remedies were underpinned by a narrative of institutional racism using gender violence as a reason to increase controls on migrants. As a result, this law has few operational measures, and an absence of preventative or educational measures.

Recent Italian legislation includes gender violence in name, but attention to GRV is limited. Most legislation is penal and addresses specific aspects, such as sexual abuse, DV and trafficking. In these laws, agency is attributed only to security forces and magistrates, while other social actors are described using gender-neutral expressions (Alldred and David 2015: 19). LGBT people are never directly mentioned and GRV is an issue solely for heterosexual people. The voices of the Italian feminist movement have been ignored in this conservative legalistic approach (ibid.: 20).

The socialist government in Spain (2004–11) set the scene for a progressive turn in legislation, with a number of laws enacted to address feminist, gender and LGBT concerns (Zabala 2009). These addressed GRV, same-sex marriage, gender reassignment, equality between men and women, and more rights over sexual and reproductive health. These laws were underpinned by a discourse that identified gender inequality as the cause of GRV. The efforts of the present conservative government (sometimes using the economic crisis as an excuse) to restrict sexual and reproductive rights and gender equality (Biglia and Olivella-Quintana 2014) have resulted in a return to a 'domestic violence' framework for understanding GRV (Bustello and Lombardo 2012).

Of the four countries reviewed through the GAP project, Spain has the greatest number of laws to address GRV explicitly. The legal approach is not just penal but also includes social measures about equality, the civil code, social services, health, immigration, education and universities, and employment. Nevertheless, the language used for framing the legislation differs between gender-neutral and gender-differentiated. But the Spanish legislative landscape is complicated by a high level of regional autonomy, with territorial autonomy in matters such as education, health and social services. For example, the Catalan government had juridical autonomy for the aspects of the GAP project on challenging GRV.

Whereas in national Spanish legislation GRV is articulated as perpetrated by men on women within a couple relationship, devolved Catalan law adopts a more feminist-informed approach that recognizes broader gendered power inequalities, with GRV recognized as also occurring in non-couple settings, although (cis or trans) women are the only recognized targets. Catalan law also recognizes a range of perpetrators that can include institutions and their board members, although in practice these are never explicitly named as offenders.

There are other differences between Catalan and Spanish legislation, with the former recognizing the importance of civil society in addressing GRV and acknowledging young people as agents with specific needs. A draft piece of legislation against LGBT discrimination in Catalonia acknowledges intersectionality, noting the interactions between homosexuality, bisexuality and transsexuality, as well as other inequalities that produce discrimination (Alldred and David 2015: 21). This high level of regional autonomy made possible the existence of multiple state and regional legislation in relation to the aspects approached by the GAP project; however, the penal code is fully regulated at the state level.

Concluding Comments

Over the last 150-year period, there have been enormous changes in women's rights and women's socio-legal positioning, not only in the global North but also the global South, or across the UN and in relation to not only what is now known as gender equality but also GRV. But VAWG and GRV still persist.

We have shown how moves from women's political equality, such as through suffrage, have gained pace and traction, first in the postwar period, from 1945, and, second, from 1995. The postwar period could be characterized as one of social democracy across the global North, when women's equality morphed into gender equality. It now appears as a 'blip' in that history. There were very significant moves towards neoliberalism at the end of the twentieth century and more recently these moves have begun to include addressing GRV across the globe, at both individual and state levels.

In the twenty-year period 1995–2015, in most of the European legislation reviewed, the specific experiences of young people and LGBT communities have been underplayed, with English law the exception in now recognizing GRV within same-sex couples (Alldred and Biglia 2015). The Spanish and Catalan laws acknowledge social responsibility for GRV, stipulate the importance of a wider range of preventative measures and introduce some intersectionality, but the analysis of the problem is not approached with the same sensibility. Although introducing some intersectionality, many aspects of Spanish law are retrogressive.

We conclude from this that legal action to combat GRV among the EU member nations that partner in this is altogether patchy and confusing and, in the recent global crisis, has been regressive. Our analysis confirms Htun and Weldon's (2012: 548) conclusion that 'the autonomous mobilization of feminists in domestic and transnational contexts . . . is the critical factor accounting for policy change . . . *[and the] impact of global norms on domestic policy making is conditional on the presence of feminist movements in domestic contexts'* (my emphasis).

We also conclude that, whereas progress in developing legal frameworks to address GRV has been made, this has mostly been within a framework of multi-layered discrimination rather than an intersectional perspective, and has failed largely to address the impact of social inequalities upon people's lives (Strid, Walby and Armstrong 2013; Gonalons-Pons and Marx Ferree 2014). This, at the very least, establishes the case for developing more education training in national contexts (Alldred and David 2015: 24).

Moreover, since the UK General Election of 2015, the broad question of human rights and the broad framework of EU and international issues around the EU Convention on Human Rights are being called into question by the newly elected Conservative government. This is part of the questioning of the place of the UK within Europe and of the EU as a constraint on the UK's so-called sovereignty and independence. Currently, the debate about whether to withdraw or to renegotiate the terms of the UK membership revolves around financial and political independence. It does not entail discussion of equal, civil and human rights but, from this perspective, the EU appears to have had a benign influence on issues of gender equality and popular feminism in the UK. How similar or different is feminist activism in the twenty-first century from its origins in second-wave feminism in the twentieth century as it began to enter the academy?

Part II

Feminist Waves about Gender Equalities and Gender Violence

4

Changing Political Landscapes of Feminism

Waves and Educational Values

Introduction

In the second decade of the twenty-first century there is a huge range of feminist tendencies across the globe. Some are incorporated into neoliberalism, while others are progressive and oppositional. To what extent these tendencies constitute a new wave of feminism, drawing from the lessons of the first and second waves, is debatable, and is the subject of this chapter. I will address evidence from my study of feminist educators and academics to try to gauge distinctive tendencies. Additionally, I want to consider how influential feminism has been in developing new educational strategies, and also how empowering it has been to women through their own learning, whether in the academy or outside.

Nevertheless higher education (HE), like the wider context within which it is situated, has been changing towards a culture characterized by 'laddism' as regards students, or a 'lad culture', which is also typified by a misogynist or sexist approach within HE management and leadership. Drawing on this evidence, from academia, I also want to consider educational or pedagogical strategies for the future. After reviewing the educational trajectories of the three cohorts of women that I studied, I will return to consider educational or training strategies or pedagogies, addressing questions of gender equality and gender-related violence (GRV).

The chapter is based upon my study about 'waves of feminism' within HE (David 2014). I interviewed over 100 international feminist educators, involved in both academia and activism, about their views of the changing contexts of HE and the wider sociopolitical systems. The vast majority of these women – and they were all chosen self-consciously as being women – felt that feminism was both a political and an educational project. The women I spoke with were all products of the global transformations of HE, becoming academic feminists and aiming to further transform academe and the wider society.

There is no sense in which my study has captured the voices of those who might be considered, as Banks (1986) noted, the *leaders* of the women's liberation movement (WLM) or even of academic feminism. Rather, I have a rich and diverse spread of feminist educators and academics, including ones who saw the obstacles rather than opportunities for creative endeavour in HE. It demonstrates the rapidly changing landscape of HE over the last fifty years, especially in terms of women's involvement and being 'first-in-the-family' (UK term) or 'first-generation' (US term) to university and/or working class. I let the women decide whether or not they considered themselves feminists, and the meanings that they attributed to this and the now commonly used notion of gender equality.

Following Banks (1986), I grouped the women into broad age cohorts, to understand their origins, actions and activities in becoming feminists in academe: what were their values and lives? They were from what Martin (2013) calls the 'breakthrough generation' and beyond, with a heritage to impart. By drawing on the voices of the three age cohorts, all of which cover both the years of birth and, some twenty years later, involvement in university or college education, I captured their views and values. Unlike Banks' or Martin's studies, all of the women I talked to were involved in universities, and it is important to capture not only their birth dates, but also timings with respect to expansions of HE. Academic capitalism is a major context, as is the rise of feminist sociology and education across the globe (David 2014: 56).

Life Histories of Feminists and Waves of Activism

In thinking through the role of feminist activism and campaigning for legislative changes, I developed a life history of feminists involved in academe, creating a collective biography as a form of participatory action research. It also served to link activism with academic work and to consider how second-wave feminism has become intimately linked with HE. Indeed, it is likely that the knowledge and evidence for campaigning derives from academic studies, within and outside of academia.

This approach, linked as it is with biographies, narratives and storytelling, is part of the 'biographic turn'. As Clare Hemmings (2006) argues:

> we need to start our histories of academic feminism from an assumption of difference and contest, an attention to subordinate as well as dominant knowledge in the present, to open up a range of possible futures rather than predictable outcomes . . . we must adopt a reflexive approach that interrogates the relationship between the histories of feminist theory that we tell and our own intellectual biographies. Nostalgia cannot be the ground of any meaningful life, still less one committed to political and collective transformation. (2006: 28–9)

She goes on to argue that individual intellectual biographies and life histories are also vital for how we, as feminists, might want to create new pedagogies, courses, curricula and, especially, feminist knowledge in the neoliberal global university.

Townsend and Weiner (2011: 141–9) argue that collective biography or what is now sometimes known as 'prosopography', 'inspired by the noted French sociologist Pierre Bourdieu [,] has become a powerful research approach . . . and has paralleled the increased interest in biography as a research source, and the wish to connect individual action with social structure' (2011: 142). They also mention pertinently Banks' work on British feminism, where she had created an account based upon feminist *activists* rather than sympathizers (ibid.: 144). Weiner (2008) had previously written engagingly about Banks' 'least "fashionable" work – her engagement with collective biography and narrative . . . this research was indeed "pioneering" – not least because it used biography systematically as a method of reversing historians' amnesia on women's participation in social and political movements' (2008: 403).

This study is also an account of women's participation in campaigns to transform women's political and socio-economic lives. Building upon Banks' important legacy, I talked to academic feminists in the humanities and social sciences, drawing on international scholars in the global North, and used feminist approaches to reflect upon individual biographies and life histories (David 2014: 52–3).

Discourses about Feminism and Gender

Early women's rights campaigners used the term 'feminism' until well into the twentieth century, but once universal suffrage was achieved, the term fell into abeyance. First-wave feminists came to be seen as rather old-fashioned 'bluestockings', with their continued campaigning for socio-political and socio-economic changes. There were, as we have seen, several outstanding international women who pursued feminist goals, including within academe – notably, for example, Alva Myrdal – but these were the exception rather than the rule.

In the 1960s, alongside civil and human rights movements, WLM arose, extending beyond simple electoral equality. This movement captured the imagination of countless groups of women, across an array of topics, from equal education, to economic equality, to sexual equality, legal and financial independence, and freedom from violence. Nevertheless, in the 1960s and 1970s, the terms 'feminism' and 'gender' were not routinely available for radical and progressive use and, indeed, had to be reinvented. The increasing use of both illustrates how quickly the momentum for such change developed.

Feminist pedagogies were also relatively unknown fifty years ago, as was the 'feminist canon'. Neither the notion of feminism nor that of gender was in the academic lexicon. These terms began to be re-created, as did the knowledge and curricula for teaching about them. This was what came to constitute feminist pedagogies and practices. Developing the theories around social and sexual divisions, and women's consciousness of these deep structures and norms, formed a substantial part of feminist knowledge and scholarship.

At the same time women were also actively creating their own ways of challenging these notions, through consciousness-raising (CR) groups, as well as through the WLM. It was only much later that ideas about 'gender norms' – relations between men and women or boys and girls in everyday practices that may include sexual abuse and harassment, bullying and more extreme forms of GRV – and gender consciousness were developed.

Feminism entered the lexicon first, followed by gender rather than sexual divisions or sex inequality somewhat later. This was a slow and contentious process amongst different and differently associated groups of feminists. These ranged from socialist or Marxist feminists, to liberal and radical feminists, with different notions about the origins of women's oppression or subordination. These also led to different approaches to campaigning for WL and/or sexual equality. It was through the development of the social sciences that distinctions came to be seen and used between sex and gender. Sex increasingly became used for either the biological distinction between men and women or the act of copulation, whereas gender increasingly has been used regarding the social differences between men and women, or their social construction from a material base as categories of difference or around identities.

The British feminist sociologist Ann Oakley was one of the first to popularize the distinction between the two, in her aptly named

Sex and Gender (Oakley 1972). But it was over a decade later that the twin terms were used less interchangeably and more distinctly. As the twentieth century drew to a close, these binary distinctions were further complicated by homosexuality, bisexuality, trans-sexuality or transgender questions. Transitions between these and issues around sexual identities came to play a stronger and more controversial part in forms of feminism linked with activism and theoretical niceties. Deborah Cameron and Joan Scanlon (2010) provide a more detailed discussion of feminist ideas about gender, which looks at their history and at what is shared by different currents within feminisms today.

By the time that the feminist journal *Gender and Education* was established in the 1980s, the language and discourse of gender equality had reached the lexicon of academia. This journal was specifically for feminist-teacher educators and for educational researchers. The creation of the UK Gender and Education Association (GEA) at the turn of the twenty-first century was a momentous event for feminist educators, coming out of years of feminist activism amongst teachers, teacher educators based within universities, and amongst other social scientists who were also feminist-activist educators in universities. The association emerged from amongst feminists who were active in creating the journal *Gender and Education*, and from a whole slew of networks, organizations and journals within British universities and in association with international networks of feminist educators.

The American Educational Research Association (AERA) – a huge international network and professional association of American educators primarily – was particularly prominent in giving impetus to feminist and gender-equality organizations. This took place alongside the growth of the social sciences in the second half of the twentieth century, and the professions associated with such developments. The UK Academy of Social Sciences was created at the turn of the twenty-first century too, illustrating these specifically British developments and the bringing together of over forty professional associations.

Feminism, Scholarly Journals and Publications

Several journals and annual conferences were also established during this era of the growth of the social sciences, and the critical perspectives associated with these. 'Feminism' rapidly joined the ranks of these critical perspectives as the term entered the academic lexicon, during the course of the 1970s. At that time, however, it was still largely in association with other progressive, radical or socialist approaches. Initially, the notion of women's studies or sexual equality within and across the disciplines was tentatively raised as an alternative to traditional approaches, in which the masculine or male predominated. Male domination, or patriarchy as it then became known, remains the bedrock of HE today despite the plethora of critiques.

The journal *Signs: Journal of Women in Culture and Society* was the first international journal of women's studies to be established in the US in 1975. Founded by the University of Chicago Press, with Catherine Stimpson of Barnard College as the founding editor, it strove to be independent of subjects and disciplines. At the forefront of new directions in feminist scholarship and inter-disciplinarity, it addressed gender, race, culture, class, nation and sexuality. At the same time, professional associations also began to develop their own critical subject journals, for example, in the US through AERA.

In the UK, the *British Journal of the Sociology of Education* (*BJSE*) was established by a group of entrepreneurial sociologists of educa-tion, including feminists such as Olive Banks, to fill a gap in the market for the sociology of education. The *Journal of Education Policy* (*JEP*) was established as a rival organization a decade or so later, while *Critical Social Policy* was established by a socialist col-lective including feminists, around the same time as *BJSE*. The Conference of Socialist Economists (CSE) also organized an annual conference and journal publications.

Other feminist journals and magazines only loosely associated with specific organizations were also created during this era, most notably *Feminist Review*, from a collective of socialist feminists, and the contrasting radical feminist magazine *Trouble and Strife*, both still going strong albeit with a changing online presence some forty years later. Similarly, women's and feminist resources, materials and books also began to proliferate.

First, the Fawcett Library – created by first-wave feminists in the 1920s – changed its name, becoming the Women's Library in the 1980s, and eventually acquiring its own tailor-made premises as part of first City Polytechnic and later the London Metropolitan University (LMU) in the late 1990s. In 2013 LMU transferred all the books and archives, but not the building, to the London School of Economics (LSE).

Parallel to this essentially women's history library, which also organized events and talks, other women, radical feminists, developed the women's research and resources centre (WRCC) in the late 1970s, which became known as the Feminist Library in the 1990s. It has continued as both an archival resource and a campaigning organization into the twenty-first century. In particular, a group known as London 1970s Sisters was reconvened and re-established through the Feminist Library in 2013, and has continued to meet regularly and campaign for feminist issues. The British Library and the Women's Library, together with the University of Sussex, also developed an archival collection of oral histories of the WLM, which was launched in 2013 (David 2014: ix).

Second-Wave Feminism 'Breaks on the Shores of Academe'

Feminist activism within the academy thus takes many forms, especially around critiques and women's studies, rather than being about education or learning per se. Second-wave feminism tends to be associated with the growth of the WLM from the 1960s, also referring to the era when women entered the academy either as students or as teachers and researchers. Whether or not it remains the same with the same values and commitments as feminisms in the present day is contestable.

Kathy Davis and Mary Evans, as editors of the *European Journal of Women's Studies*, were interested in the trajectories of feminist theories amongst generations of scholars in the global academy. Davis and Evans (2011), as sociologists, invited their contributors to think about a 'feminist canon', drawing upon the US by contrast with European and/or British ideas. The contributors all produced autobiographical reflective essays, grouped around three overlapping themes, to structure their book, namely: (i) becoming a feminist in a transatlantic context (largely the US and the UK); (ii) activism inside and outside the academy; and (iii) theoretical engagements.

They argued that:

> while we can now recognize the paradox of the unity of difference, there remains the reality of difference. As feminists we have come together and built on shared ideas and traditions. We have gendered the human, but with that comes the question of the limits of humanism; in demonstrating . . . the limitations of identities of generation and geography, we now have to ask how we begin to work on the politics (be they academic or otherwise) of that humanism which feminism has made possible. To what extent . . . are we prepared to accept the possible disruptions and discontinuities that an extended conversation on difference might encounter[?] (Davis and Evans 2011: 221)

Similarly, a group of Canadian feminist scholars put together reflections on feminist work entering the academy, entitled *Minds of Their Own: Inventing Feminist Scholarship and Women's Studies in Canada and Quebec, 1966–1976* (Robbins et al. 2008). This makes clear how the contributors were all from the generation of second-wave feminism. Two of the editors, namely Margrit Eichler and Meg Luxton, show the importance of preserving the memories of the heydays of feminist involvement in creating new knowledge and wisdom for global education. One of their contributors, Lorna Marsden, also wrote an essay with the extremely apposite title 'Second-Wave Feminism Breaks on the Shores of U of T'.

Most recently, a presentation at the biennial conference of the GEA, held in London in 2015 at Roehampton University, alerted me to the continuing appeal of investigating such trajectories of feminist academics. Three Brazilian feminist academics from the University of Paraiba – Maria Eulina P. de Carvalho, Gloria Raby and Flavia Maia Guimaraes – presented a collective biography of trajectories of feminist academics in north and north-east Brazil, mainly around Recife. They concentrated on a group of women from the age cohort of 1930–60 and considered how they established a feminist network of gender studies and gender studies research centres. They also considered obstacles and opportunities for such developments amongst the women as students and professionals in academe. They argued that 'activism was the key to the women's academic identification'. They also considered the role of social and university movements for change as central to the women's identities and their strategies for empowerment.

All of this work maps on to my study of three generations of feminist educators in academe. The conclusions of these three different types of study also compare with mine in that it is argued that much has been achieved, especially around issues of gender and race equality for the women themselves, but there have been limitations in the extent of influence in government policies and practices. The three Brazilian women concluded that change through Federal programmes in Brazil remained 'a distant dream'.

Feminism, Gender and Universities

I dubbed many of my interviewees 'education feminists', borrowing the term from the American Lynda Stone's *The Education Feminism Reader* (1994), or 'academic feminists'. Initially, my aim was to interview self-styled feminists involved in teaching and research in academia, mainly of my generation born in the shadows of the war, and who had entered academe some two or three decades later.

I spread my net widely over the various networks and international associations with which I was loosely associated. I started with the networks of feminists and women that I knew from my initial political and professional associations, such as through the Bristol Women's Studies Group (BWSG), celebrating the thirtieth anniversary of the publication of our *Half The Sky: An Introduction to Women's Studies* (1979). I augmented this with other professional associations, using the snowball technique.

When I decided not to confine myself to my generation, I approached younger generations. These tended to be associated more with education and the sociology of education, so-called 'education feminists', than my earlier networks of 'academic feminists' concerned largely with social policy, sociology and women's studies. I asked all the women if they would prefer to reply in writing by email or be interviewed. The vast majority decided to reply by email to a set of questions that I had provided (David 2014: 193–4), although I also had some key interviews with pertinent international feminist scholars. The participants wanted to be named and acknowledged, rather than remaining anonymous. In the event, I obtained a far larger number of women and their voices than I had initially anticipated.

I obtained over 100 international participants in my study, from across three generations or cohorts. These women are in no sense representative of all feminist academics and educators. Rather, mine is a partial study: partial in the sense that it illustrates my own personal and political commitment to feminism, feminist scholarship and knowledge, particularly around women's studies or gender equality. It is also partial in that it is a qualitative study of three generations or cohorts of women, committed to either feminism or gender equality in education, and especially higher education. Nevertheless, while it only covers three cohorts, it also highlights how critical to women's lives feminism, feminist scholarship and feminist pedagogy has been. Also, given that my third cohort or generation were all born before 1980, this means that I effectively excluded younger women, and women who might consider themselves third- or fourth-wave feminists. Emily Henderson, who has undertaken imaginative feminist educational work through her *Gender Pedagogy* (Henderson 2015), pointed this out most clearly: the resurgence of popular feminism also illustrates my limitations.

Cohorts of Academic or Education Feminists

Given my initial approach, the vast majority of my participants, whether now based in the UK or elsewhere in the global North, were from my generation or cohort (1935 to 1950). Over half of all my participants were in this first cohort, although not all were involved in developing feminist educational studies, but were associated with women's studies and critiques of the traditional disciplines. Larger numbers of my later and smaller cohorts (women born between 1950 and 1965; and between 1965 and 1980 respectively) were more clearly involved with feminist educational studies and specifically gender and education.

Overall, most of my participants turned out to be professors in the US sense of being 'full' professors (although, in the UK, not necessarily tenured). This applied to almost three-quarters of all the 110 women, and the other participants were in relatively senior positions as academics or researchers, with a tiny number having left academe for more activist and policy pursuits. My study was made up of a diversity of women academics, across the generations and ages, and also extremely varied in terms of their social and geographic locations: illustrative of the mobile, transnational academics who are characteristic of the overall academic profession in the twenty-first century (Kim and Brooks 2013; David 2014: 17). While most of the participants were resident in the UK, many were not born here but came from former British colonies such as Australia, Canada, the

Table 4.1 Participants from networks of international feminists

Current country of residence	Totals	Cohort 1 (1935–1950)	Cohort 2 (1950–1965)	Cohort 3 (1965–1980)
Australasia	5	5		
Canada	7	6	1	
India/Israel/Spain	3	1	1	1
Ireland	2		1	1
UK	83	45	28	10
US	10	9	1	
TOTALS	**110**	**66**	**32**	**12**

Caribbean, India, Pakistan, South Africa and the US, and other parts of Europe – France, Greece, Spain (David 2014: 18).

The two older cohorts were senior members of the academy, many of whom had already retired (and indeed some of the women interviewed have since passed away), illustrating the urgency of the project of developing a life history and collective biography of second-wave feminisms. Even my youngest cohort, being born between 1965 and 1980, are now so-called senior or mid-career women. One of my participants of this youngest cohort, namely Dr Kelly Coate (Coate, Howson and Croix 2015), has undertaken an explicitly feminist study, funded by the Leadership Foundation for Higher Education in the UK, of such mid-career women, allowing the participants to self-define what is meant by career and by being in the middle of such a career, while also linking the study to indicators of prestige within and across academia. Many of the participants could now be seen as potentially fourth-wave feminists.

I did not target particular individuals, institutions or professional associations but, given my own research interests and predilections, it is not surprising that my partial study has many participants who see themselves as feminist-activist educators or academics. Many of them were either in the GEA, or in cognate organizations such as the AERA. 'Education feminists' is the term that I have used to group those who are committed to and publishing in feminist studies of education and gender. Across my three cohorts, I identified over half of the women from the first cohort as being 'education feminists', with over three-quarters from the second cohort and the vast majority of the youngest cohort being identified as part this group. However, of this substantial group of 'education feminists', there are significant differences between them in their origins and approaches to feminism, gender and education.

The Social and Educational Origins of Feminist Academics

Clearly, there are striking differences between the women in their social class backgrounds, and I decided to use notions drawn from the women's accounts of themselves, rather than any objective notion. Given that all the women are social scientists and have been involved in considerations of social class and social mobility in their own work, they had sophisticated and nuanced understandings of these questions (David 2014: 85). Family backgrounds are defined not only by parents' social class as being about income (or means), but also by their occupations, with many of the women having parents who were either schoolteachers or university professors. This turned out to be significantly higher than expected, especially in relation to 'education feminists'.

Indeed, one of the major transformations of HE over the last fifty years, responsible for the increasing numbers of women as students in HE, has been the incorporation of teacher education as an undergraduate study, with different patterns across different countries. Many of the participants also had parents, mothers especially, who had participated in teacher education, not then named as HE, and so were not (technically) 'first-in-the-family' or 'first generation' to go to university, though they felt it to be so.

Notions of social class vary slightly across the countries, with working class not common in the US, but an American feminist from the middle cohort used it for her father whereas her mother was a teacher:

> My father was a construction worker, and my mother was a teacher before she became pregnant with me (I was told that when she married, she was told by the principal of her school that were she to get pregnant she would lose her job, which indeed she did) ... *My parents' marriage 'crossed' class* in this sense, and religion (my father raised a Catholic and mother raised a Baptist). (my emphasis; David 2014: 87)

Another, now a Canadian citizen but originally from the US, and from the first cohort, said:

> My parents were teachers, although my mother stopped work when she was pregnant with me, and did not go back to teaching. She was a physical education teacher and my dad was an art teacher. He taught in elementary and junior high schools when I was young, then

Table 4.2 Social class families (including parental education) across the three cohorts

Social class distribution	Cohort 1 (1935–1950)	Cohort 2 (1950–1965)	Cohort 3 (1965–1980)	Totals
Upper/upper middle class	22	7	3	32 (29%)
Middle/lower middle class	30	13	5	48 (45%)
Working class	14	12	4	30 (27%)
TOTALS	**66**	**32**	**12**	**110**

moved into high school teaching for most of his career . . . Both of my parents had bachelor's degrees . . . Additionally my father had a master's degree in educational administration . . . for which he took courses part-time at night . . . I also remember him teaching summer school courses in English and history, as teachers in those days did not make much money. 'Teachers' salaries' were always bemoaned as low . . . My dad had been upwardly mobile by becoming a teacher, as his parents were Jewish immigrants from Poland and his father worked in a factory. My mother was slightly downwardly mobile, as her family was well established in Detroit and her father and grandfather were businessmen. The Depression affected both their families and their own lives as young people. (David 2014: 89)

Another Canadian wrote about her 'working-class family':

My father worked for the government. I remember that money was short but my mother couldn't work outside our home – government policy. When I was six, she returned as a bookkeeper . . . My mother graduated from high school but my father had had to go into 'service' when he was approx. sixteen ('under-footman'), then immigrated to Canada. Dad had been offered a scholarship for high school but his mother (much married, often single parent, housekeeper) told him, according to family myth, that 'his family was working class, always had been working class and always would be working class'. Dad finished high school in Canada, rode the rails to Vancouver, and was unemployed for several years. It was the height of the Depression.

Table 4.3 First-in-the-family or first generation to go to university

First-in-the-family and social class	Cohort 1 (1935–1950)	Cohort 2 (1950–1965)	Cohort 3 (1965–1980)	Totals
Working class	14	12	4	30 (27%)
Middle class first-in-the family	12	9	4	25 (23%)
Total first-in-the-family	26 (39%)	21 (66%)	8 (75%)	55 (50%)

Money was available for training as a radio operator, so he became a radio operator. Finally he got a job and he and Mum could get married. (David 2014: 89)

Given the expansion of HE, many from rather privileged middle-class backgrounds were 'first-in-the-family' or at very least 'first girl'. Thus, my study demonstrated considerable social mobility amongst the three cohorts, linked as it was to transformations in HE. Many of my participants volunteered this information, although I had not specifically asked them to (David 2014: 81).

Overall, only a little over a quarter claimed to be from working-class families, whereas nearly double said they were 'first-in-the-family'. This clearly illustrates how the expansion of HE, specifically to include women's traditional professions such as teacher education and social work, has become part of the expanded university. It also produces very interesting class trends across the three cohorts, with proportionately more from the working class in cohorts two and three than in cohort one. Equally, there has been a growth in the proportions of 'first-in-the-family' middle class in cohorts two and three. Only one in five of cohort one participants said they were working class, whereas twice as many said they were 'first-in-the-family', although occasionally this refers only to being the 'first-*girl*-in-the-family'.

The working-class 'first-in-the-family' are more clear-cut, with examples like those planning to be teachers. One Australian said: 'mine is definitely a working-class family . . . father was a milkman (brought up on a small dairy farm), mother a mender in a woollen mill (or full-time housewife). Both left school at minimum age (fourteen)' (p. 91). Another said: 'Working-class family, oldest of eight siblings. Father left school at thirteen to become a coalminer, mother left school at sixteen to work in the office of a factory but became a housewife on marriage' (p. 91). Another American said that she was 'born into a second-generation working-class Italian-Franco-American family where neither of my parents completed high school' (p. 92).

Two-thirds of cohort two said they were 'first-in-the-family', while only a third said they were working class. Examples of the range of middle-class families are: 'No one had been to university before me . . . father worked in a small flooring company; mother a primary school teacher' (p. 92).

> Neither of my parents went to university, but both had full secondary education. In a different generation my mother would certainly have progressed to university – after taking the Leaving Certificate she worked in the civil service until she got married. Later in life, she attended university extra-mural courses in a range of subjects (including philosophy) and took some pride in being a 'university student'. (p. 92)

> I was the eldest girl and in the end my parents had six children (in the space of seven years!) . . . My father trained to be a priest . . . but decided against it the year he was due to be ordained . . . my mother was from a large Catholic family. *Neither parent went to university but my mum trained to be a primary school teacher.* My father used wireless skills learned at the end of the war to get into computer engineering. He worked for IBM for most of his life. (p. 92)

Working-class families in cohort two included: 'Born . . . to young parents (mum nineteen and dad twenty-one). Mother's background upper working class; father's lower working class. We all lived with my grandparents until I was five when my parents got a council flat . . . both parents left school at minimum age', 'an upper-working-class family . . . nobody in the family had been to university' (p. 92); 'I was born into a working-class family. My father was a manual worker in an oil refinery, my mother a house-wife' (p. 92).

Parents were both working class, but aspirational middle class. *Neither went to HE.* Father wanted to and gained entrance qualifications, but his parents sent him out to work as they needed his income. It was a lifelong hurt for him that he wasn't able to be a lawyer. He was an insurance manager, but also did very well during the war and rose to the rank of major. My mother was half Maltese and immigrated to the UK when she was thirteen – very bright, but absolutely no educational opportunities. She married young and had my sister when she was twenty. All my mother's creativity went into the home – cooking, gardening, dressmaking, etc. – very Catholic! (p. 92)

Skilled working-class family – I was the *first to go to University.* My father was a tool-maker and my mother was a bus conductor and then owned a café (she came from a family of shop owners). My brother was expelled from school at fifteen, married and emigrated to Australia, divorced and returned . . . My sister also left school at fifteen and went into a factory. (p. 92)

Very poor working-class family, eldest of five siblings. My father left school at fourteen and worked as an unskilled labourer for most of his life – his longest job was in an abattoir. My mother left school at fifteen, married at nineteen, and worked first as a factory worker and then a secretary. We lived in rented flats and then on a rough council estate. No one in my family had been to grammar school, let alone university. (p. 92)

Finally, two of the women from black and minority ethnic groups (BME) told of their similar Caribbean influences. One was 'born to a peasant family (mother a nurse and midwife; father an electrician; *neither parent went to university*) in the Caribbean' (p. 89), whereas the other's education was more mixed as she had Trinidadian teachers:

My mum is Austrian and my father was Indo-Caribbean. They met in London . . . I was born in 1958 . . . and my brother is a year older than me. It was the 1950s, the whole period of no dogs, no Irish, no blacks – it was a very difficult time for both of them. So we went to live in

Trinidad when I was four years old. I was schooled up until sixteen in Trinidad. (p. 91)

A quarter of cohort three said they were working class, while three-quarters were 'first-in-the-family'. Examples of working-class families are:

> My father was a first-generation Irish immigrant (Catholic) who worked in the wholesale fruit and veg trade. My mother was a Protestant, born in the English Midlands to market traders . . . My mother worked all her working life as a seamstress in a factory . . . My parents separated when I was six. *I was the first and am still the only member of my family to go to university.* (p. 93)

> The third child of three . . . My father, around that time, worked as a labourer for his father who owned a quarry. Later my dad became a hospital porter . . . My mum did not undertake paid work when I was a small child . . . I'd describe my family as working class, although partly because of my grandfather's relative wealth from his business, we lived in what was a middle-class area, in a relatively large house, with a large garden, large car, etc. So, overall, I'd say definitely working class in terms of 'cultural capital' but with a middle-class home, etc. My parents placed a lot of value on education for us as children. Both parents left school at the end of compulsory schooling. (p. 93)

Finally, a Spanish academic was: 'Working class – I am "first generation" in my family at university except an aunt (mother's sister) who is a doctor,' (p. 92) while an American simply said that her parents were artists with *no university*.

Feminist University Pioneers

All this shows that the global expansion of HE has indeed allowed *more opportunities for women as students*. The women themselves tell nuanced stories about their education and social transformations and of their formation in, for example, Catholic, Protestant, Jewish and/or BME families. It is clear from this brief analysis that over the three cohorts most participants are not from privileged social and family backgrounds, but have been *pioneers in creating HE for themselves and subsequent generations*. This has not necessarily been a simple or easy path. One said: 'As a faculty member I was pulled by socialist feminist theories and associated empirical research. My family was not impressed with my move towards radical politics in general nor feminism more specifically. They in fact took issue with who I was becoming both intellectually and personally' (David 2014: 94).

Education Feminists: Complex Career Strategies Linked to Social Class?

Many of cohort one went to university straight from school to do an undergraduate degree and then undertook research or pursued an academic career, while others then qualified as postgraduate teachers and went into school-teaching, before returning to higher education many years later. A substantial number of this cohort, as with cohort two, qualified as teachers first, through attending a teacher training college, or college of education (at that time outside the university sector).

The pattern for the third cohort is interestingly different, despite its small size. The vast majority of the education feminists have pursued academic careers, including research, with only one becoming a schoolteacher first. Indeed, one mentioned starting off by pursuing primary school-teaching only to transfer to doing a master's and then a doctorate, after she had found the teaching course not to her satisfaction. In my discussion of what the various education feminists had said about their origins and initial training, I noted that many saw this as part of the process of social and educational mobility (David 2014: 81–2).

Overall, and across all the countries, a fifth of the participants – all now professors – *initially trained as teachers*. The majority came from cohort one with less than a third from cohort two. The older women who trained as teachers had varied routes into and from teaching, although for the most part they undertook undergraduate studies, followed by teacher education. Twelve from cohort one had trained as graduates, such as the ones from the Antipodes, from Israel, the US and the UK.

Some in England had trained initially at college – because much teacher education, at that time, was not included in universities – before teaching and later moving into teacher education. This was also, as one put it, a *class* choice, being from a working-class family. Whether trained initially at college or university, several from cohort one started off as primary schoolteachers. Another from cohort two, from a working-class family, did primary teacher training, taught and then obtained a degree from the Open University, before doing her doctorate.

One of the education professors trained and worked as a teacher, and returned to academe much later, and 'didn't graduate' as she put it but 'went to Teacher Training College – needed to stay near home/ensure I could get a well-paid job so it was the "natural" route for a young woman like myself . . . [Instead] did two MAs and a PhD and a DipEd, which was fabulous' (David 2014: 81).

Another education professor similarly went to a college of education to do a BEd to become a primary school teacher:

> which I was for three years. Then I decided to do an MA . . . and thought about in the evening but decided not, as I had two young children and it was too far away. I lived in north London then . . . after my MA it was suggested that I do a PhD and I was so flattered that I started part-time PhD on girls and maths . . . However, I couldn't sustain it, and it was only later . . . that I decided to do a PhD. It took me eight years to complete part time . . . but eventually I got my PhD. (David 2014: 80)

Pedagogical Predilections and Doctoral 'Education'

The three generations identified might be roughly linked with three different phases of feminist pedagogical developments in academe. These are also associated with wider developments in the expansion of the arts, humanities and social sciences in postwar universities. First, the oldest cohort was composed of university pioneers, creating feminist thought and knowledge, linked to political activism, but doing so without any formal university or educational qualifications. While coming to feminism during their student years, none studied feminism in their coursework but outside and through their reading.

Although the vast majority of my participants have doctorates, either a PhD or a DPhil, or an education doctorate (EdD), or PhD by publication, this also varies across the three cohorts. All of cohort three have some kind of doctorate, mostly on feminist topics, and are mainly professional educators; only one of cohort two does not have a doctorate but is a professor; but there are ten of cohort one who do not have doctorates (including both professors and non-professors, or senior researchers). The reasons for this are, indeed, to do with both the changing nature of HE and women's changing place within it, as well as the subjects taken, and the fact that a large proportion of my participants are in education. For several of cohorts one and two, gaining a doctorate occurred later in life, either on returning to HE or because other social and family factors intervened. Indeed, it is quite clear that these trajectories are rather typical of women's lives for this generation and indicate clearly where feminist pedagogies became paramount.

A distinguished researcher on family policy and domestic violence, from Australia, is one of the four from the first cohort who was neither a professor nor a doctor (although she has an honorary doctorate from Bristol):

I worked as a teacher while doing an MA . . . I came to Bristol because my husband was offered a fellowship in the Physics Department. Here I started an ambitious MPhil/PhD . . . failed to survive the difficulty of combining research, writing and motherhood in the rather hostile environment of the University of Bristol in the heyday of early Bowlbyism . . . I went back to school-teaching which was made exciting by the advent of the WLM . . . I have been pretty well immersed in feminism (and left-wing socialism) for most of my life and have always combined learning and activism, and learning THROUGH activism. (David 2014: 105)

Clearly a doctorate was not at all expected: three now very distinguished British professors of social policy did not have doctorates, and did not consider embarking upon them. There was often no pressure to complete a doctorate; for example, another feminist activist that I interviewed who was a mature undergraduate student wrote that she

> didn't get very far with the PhD. Supervision was lax and I was involved in loads of activism. I also separated from my husband and moved house . . . I wrote quite a lot however throughout the 1980s and was awarded a PhD by publication in 1990 – seven years after getting a permanent job at a new university. (David 2014: 84)

Another participant from the middle cohort wrote that: 'I started a doctorate when I got my first academic post at thirty-four, but withdrew from it because of family problems. I didn't complete my doctorate (by publication) until I was fifty-five.'

The relationships between feminist academics and graduate students in developing particular feminist approaches to the subject matter became very important for the cohort of university pioneers. Interestingly, from my study and perhaps because of my own greater involvement in education as both a discipline and a method, a large minority of the women were involved in education as a professional practice. This meant that many of them first went into school-teaching only later to return to HE, where they undertook doctorates that were feminist in topic and practice.

Feminist Teachers and Feminist Educators: The 'Education Feminists'

Kathleen Weiler, the American feminist, elaborates this picture of schoolteacher becoming teacher educator:

When I did go to graduate school to get a doctorate in education, I decided I would write a thesis that would address feminist issues. The topic of my doctoral thesis (which was later published) was on a topic dear to my heart as a feminist high-school teacher – I studied feminist high-school teachers! Politically and theoretically, I was drawn to this research because I hadn't found anything like it in the theory I was reading . . . but I still wasn't clear how to connect critical theory with my feminist concerns. In my graduate program, there were no courses addressing gender, let alone feminist educational theory, *so like many other feminist education scholars in the early 1980s I was sort of making it up as I went along.* I was aware of some education scholars who were developing a feminist analysis . . . In fact Sue Middleton in New Zealand was conducting the research for her book *Educating Feminists* at almost exactly the same time that I was doing the field work for what became *Women Teaching for Change*, but we were unaware of one another at the time. I felt I was alone with my research. I thought my task was to reconcile my feminist politics (a broad but random reading of feminist theory) with the more structured reading and analysis I was doing of (male) critical social theory and neo-Marxist educational theory . . . I also came to see the work of the women teachers I was 'studying' as more complex, particularly around questions of race and institutional power. So things became decidedly more muddied the more I hung around the schools doing fieldwork and particularly when I began to write. I think this process of seeing greater complexity was typical of second-wave feminists at this time who moved from a commitment to the political activism of the women's movement to the complexities of studying individuals in institutions and social structures. (my emphasis; David 2014: 82)

Three Australians have very similar trajectories and discuss how their doctorates were feminist in focus – with Bronwyn Davies writing:

I went to a small rural university in part because 'the city' was regarded as too dangerous by my father for girls (1961). I enrolled in a BA and DipEd as I got a 'Teachers College Scholarship' which carried with it the obligation to do five years' teaching. I wanted to study science but

having been to a small girls' private school I had not studied physics
and chemistry, which were pre-requisites . . . My first jobs were teaching in school and then later I became an academic . . . I had found my
BA utterly demoralizing and did not enrol in the DipEd until after my
marriage was over. I had thought the only thing I was competent to do
was marry and take care of husband and children . . .

After I was widowed at age twenty-five I completed a DipEd while teaching
in school and then a BEd and a PhD while teaching at university full-time and
raising my three kids. For my PhD I had a few nominal male PhD super-
visors who claimed they couldn't understand what I was writing as it
was qualitative research. I was blocked from submitting my PhD for
examination when it was completed on the grounds that they could
not assess its quality. I negotiated that it would be submitted to a high-
status outsider for evaluation. His evaluation was so positive that I was
able to submit it. It was later published as a book with Routledge. (my
emphasis; David 2014: 134)

The middle cohort in my study is composed of women who
were more clearly involved in becoming professional academics
and self-consciously integrating their feminism into their studies,
by also undertaking feminist doctorates. There are particular outstanding examples here of two now well-known black feminists,
namely Professors Ann Phoenix and Heidi Mirza. Unfortunately, I
did not manage to capture many black feminists: these two women
are relatively unique. They each wrote as follows, illustrating their
self-conscious attempts to develop feminist doctoral scholarship
within education. They also demonstrate the importance of an
aspect of the 'family-education couple', namely combining motherhood with their scholarly and activist work. They are illustrative
of this cohort's developing practices of feminist learning and
education.

Ann abandoned her first PhD, and moved to do a more
consciously feminist topic.

. . . went to St Andrews University . . . University is central . . .
I already thought of myself as a feminist at St Andrews . . . then I
went to Manchester to do psychology for an MA and followed by

a PhD that I never finished although I had a grant. I gave it up after fourteen months having left my then husband when my baby was six months old . . . By this time I had been in several feminist CR groups, starting in Scotland, and I was one of the founder members of Manchester Rape Crisis. Several things sparked an Ahha moment and Ann Oakley's *Becoming a Mother* in 1981 was one as it was the year I became a mother . . . I was involved in black politics as well as feminist politics and the two were antithetical . . . the split was occurring but I didn't feel myself split . . . Both these groups became central to my political activity and to the friendships I formed . . . it was lovely when things from black American feminists came out . . . it was just great . . . I moved to London and started a second PhD . . . on the effects of daycare on children and interviewed mothers, social workers and teachers. I observed bathtimes and mothers going back to work. *Young Mothers* was my book from my PhD. (David 2014: 134)

Heidi comes from a similar background, also having a baby while a student, but her politicization had a different trajectory:

I went to an all girls' school in Trinidad . . . High-achieving girls didn't mean careers for girls, it meant good wives for husbands! . . . there were strong female 'role models' in my early life – but they lived very traditional lives in a very patriarchal culture. Growing up in Trinidad, I was very influenced by the black power movement in the early seventies . . . When we came back to England in 1973 we lived in Brixton and I went to the local school. The racism there was incredible . . . I do think I was racialized before I was feminized! That came later at university when I got married . . . when I graduated . . . My PhD thesis was a small-scale ethnography of young Caribbean girls like myself in a London school. Because of my experience I wanted to write about the interplay between career choices and educational structures. So in a way the thesis was about my own life, it was a process of exploring the practices of racism and exclusion which I saw around me . . . My marriage was very pivotal for me as a black/postcolonial feminist. I got married in my first year of university when I was nineteen and I had my daughter as I was leaving in the third year. In fact I was very pregnant when I sat my finals! My husband was a very devout Muslim, and I wasn't! I converted to Islam during the time of the first Muslim uprisings in the seventies . . . My degree built my confidence as a woman which I had not got at school . . . there was a lot of passion and activism in what I was doing. (David 2014: 135–6)

The Education of Professional Academics as Feminists

As is clear from these illustrations from the second cohort, feminism in HE was gradually evolving into a mixture of the political and the educational, or pedagogical. These two were becoming increasingly difficult to separate. Moving to the youngest and third cohort, and those who have often been associated with third- rather than second-wave feminism, it is clearly the case that their feminist pedagogies are integrated into their becoming professional academics and activists. They all give the clearest instances of how important education, and especially feminist education, has been to their learning and becoming feminists. First, the following example is important in terms of seeing how earlier feminist activism to set up women's refuges enabled the cultivation of subsequent femi- nists on the cusp of the third wave:

> I became a feminist during university (as a mature student at Middlesex after an Access to HE course) mainly through my own reading . . . good experiences taught me about inclusive pedagogies. . . . Feminism has been crucial to my learning – indirectly and explicitly – e.g., when I was in a women's aid refuge I first explicitly encountered feminism and this was a life saver in terms of understanding and making sense of my traumatic experiences of domestic violence; and also learning about my rights and my position as a woman – this was strengthened at university when I started to read feminist theories for my coursework. Theory has been more directly influential to me than activism, which has not been a significant part of my history/experience (although I have participated in 'activism' in more modest, localized ways). (David 2014: 159)

Similarly, two other feminist-activist academics tell of how they learnt their feminist practices from their readings and their collaborative work in academe. I use these two as illustrations, again, of how the mix of activism and pedagogies was becoming inseparable and important to feminist pedagogies and practices. They are two feminists with whom I have been working on the GAP project. They see their more recent trajectories being into feminist activists in academe. Both again illustrate how feminist doctorates are a fundamental part of the process.

Fin chose her graduate and doctoral work very clearly and deliberately:

> after my undergraduate, I studied for a postgraduate qualification, a Masters in cultural studies, and then a doctorate in education. During my MA I *purposefully chose feminist and gender options* . . . I was keen to explore the gendered experiences of young women. *The academics I approached to consider supervising my work, were all active feminists, and my two supervisors were feminists with an interest in gender and education.* The PhD study came during a brief hiatus in my professional life. After completing my MA, I had tried to consolidate my professional work, and had taken work at a charity delivering drugs education in schools . . . I decided I would quit and work the summer on playschemes. Luckily, I noted a scholarship and thought it might be a good idea to develop my proposal and see if I might have a chance. I did, and the scholarship enabled me to commit to my PhD studies, and resulting change in direction in my professional life. (my emphasis; David 2014: 157)

Pam undertook her PhD in psychology, supervised by academic feminists, 'on parenting, family and feminism'. She said that she wavered about becoming a feminist:

> Part at uni, part afterwards . . . Straight after uni I moved to London, into an ex-student household of uni psych graduates, one of whom would become my first girlfriend and who lent me feminist texts and feminist psychology textbooks. *A profound politicization occurred then [including an] evangelical enthusiasm about my newfound lesbianism, was*

never quite radical feminist but had strands of/was influenced by. Awareness of 'the male in the head' and heterosexualization of everyday life was profound . . . So seeds sown at uni but unfocused and untheorized. Actually *Erica Burman had a huge impact and was and is a bedazzling inspiration . . . so feminism's woven through my personal journey* which is mirrored by feminist theory journey from liberal to lesbian feminism to socialist feminism to queer theory. Feminist frameworks and politics feel the most central to me although . . . activism is important too. My journey across and between the various social sciences has been through feminist work that didn't respect the disciplinary boundaries and my finding that I could have sexuality as a legitimate research topic is down to this too. It was nice finding that the illicit reading on sexuality could be owned and legitimate. My later studies in teaching and learning (PgDip HE) looped back into feminist and queer pedagogies too . . . I tend to assume it is OK to be a feminist at work and have to be corrected sometimes. (my emphasis; David 2014: 158)

Values and Waves of Feminism Across the Generations

While feminist values were paramount in all three cohorts, the ways in which these played out in the women's lives were clearly rather different. The first cohort – the university pioneers of feminist scholarship and practice – had fewer opportunities for formal learning of feminism but far more freedom to develop forms of critical and feminist education as pedagogical practices, with the second able to integrate the gains of feminist critical scholarship in their own doctoral work and practices. Finally, the third cohort, while far more professionally schooled in feminist practices, also had to contend with a much more austere culture. This culture has been highly resistant to the embedding of emerging gender identities. Indeed, the public acceptance of the notion of gender equality is at odds with the development of a critical gender identity and practices in HE.

Given the problematic nature of the notion of waves of feminism, I decided to discuss it with all of my participants. My task was similar to the question that Nancy Hewitt (2010: xi) set herself in her 'symposium . . . thinking about histories of feminism and women's activism over many years. This project . . . allowed me the freedom to re-imagine narratives of women's history, women's rights and feminism.' In her resulting edited collection Hewitt (2010: 1) argues that 'the concept of waves surging and receding cannot fully capture these multiple and overlapping movements, chronologies, issues and sites' (David 2014: 59).

I found differences within as well as between the three cohorts of women, such that overarching feminist values shone through, although there were major differences of emphasis as these examples from amongst my international feminist educators illustrate. The wave analogy was thought to be useful by many of my participants, but it did not always relate to the notion of sea or even hair waves. One of my participants imaginatively thought of *waves* as not being about hair, but air, as in her comment that 'WLM hit the air waves just as I was entering graduate school'. Many of my participants saw Stevie Smith's poem *Not Waving But Drowning* as being a major critique of one of the several ideas behind waves rather than it being a singular notion (David 2014: 61).

The American feminist pedagogue, Frinde Maher, provided a clear and succinct summary:

> Yes . . . whom younger women call 'The Second Wave'. In spite of many of us having spent years diversifying and deconstructing our definitions of the falsely unifying term 'woman' 'Third Wavers' tend to accuse us of racism for not seeing differences among women. Also it seems to me, they are not fighting those fights for inclusion the way we did. But I could be wrong. The challenge is to use feminism as a constant tool to fight increasing inequalities across the globe, against women but also against their families and their communities. Second-Wave feminism is against inequalities in a way that I feel Third-Wave feminists, with their concern for 'the body' and transgender issues are not always. (David 2014: 61)

The Canadian feminist scholar and educator, Alison Griffith, wrote:

Yes. Not many of the new generation of academic women call themselves feminists. *It is both assumed and subsumed.* For me, it means that
the feminist academic conversation has moved away from its political
roots. I see the influence of feminism waning, overtaken by other social
justice issues. Given that gender seems to be the most difficult social distinction to moderate, and given the shift to neoliberal social conditions,
I don't find this surprising, just depressing. (David 2014: 61)

A key second-wave feminist concerned with gender and education, who has published widely on the topic of schooling and
universities – Sandra Acker – agreed that she was a second-wave
feminist:

we positioned gender/women more centrally. We drew from liberal,
socialist and radical feminisms, with their various sub-groups, and
often worked programmatically, for example espousing liberal feminist
standpoints rather than more radical ones so that something would
get done. Newer feminisms seem less action-oriented. Sexuality has
always been contentious and while second-wave feminism accepted or
embraced lesbian feminism, the idea of playing with or troubling the
idea of gender is a newer phase . . . intersectionality has taken a greater
role, so that the category of 'women' is often challenged. With that
challenge, it is difficult to do the kind of work second-wave feminism
did in educational circles in raising consciousness and working for
changes in representation and curriculum and classroom experience.
Another challenge has been the idea that feminism has done its work
and it is now underachieving boys that educators need to be concerned
about. (David 2014: 63)

And yet others tried to be 'firmly but critically from a second-
wave perspective', so that another leading British education
professor said:

I am a second-wave feminist and sociologist; I have always been
concerned to help make girls' voices heard in the public domain,
especially heard by teachers, and so I do appreciate the skills of those
who are able to uncover female identities and experiences. However,

nowadays it is worrying that teachers are no longer our audience. In the 1970s and 1980s we validated teachers as agents of change . . . as 'insider reformers'. In the 1980s we spoke directly to the teaching profession and showed them our research findings. Now it seems as if the audience for gender and education is ourselves. We have lost a lot of our audience in the profession and the worry is that we are speaking to ourselves about ourselves. I am definitely a second-waver! (David 2014: 64)

An Australian feminist was equivocal:

Yes. I did see feminism as both 'modernist' in the sense of allied to movements like Marxism, but also post-modernist, in the deconstructive aspects of it being particularly important and having value. I think that some of the further elaborations of deconstructive or poststructuralist work, and the endless taking up of Foucault, have got more jargon-laden and moved away from practical engagement . . . I have been through many of the debates about women's studies in universities and the different forms (and names) these might take. Currently the humanities and social sciences in Australia are being financially squeezed and there is much less opportunity to mount interest-driven subjects compared with big and combined ones. But I think some attention to feminist issues is quite mainstream in history, sociology. (David 2014: 64)

Sue Middleton, the New Zealand education feminist, also expressed the changes well:

I don't think of it this way, although I accept that the younger women's issues, needs, ideas, and modes of operating are quite different from those of our generation – and so they should be. Personally, I felt a huge change at menopause (after a hysterectomy at forty-six) as personal questions of reproduction, career 'stage' and motherhood (my daughter left home) were personally less immediate. My focus shifted away from gender per se and more into issues concerning the fate of educational theory in the amalgamating universities and teachers' colleges. I began researching the lives and ideas of 'old' teachers (. . .

did our oral history) – including feminists . . . Students were repelled
by feminism (it was their mothers' thing) through the late 1990s. But
now things have changed again. Present students are enthralled by 'old
feminism' but sometimes think the battles have been won. It doesn't
take much though to get them worked up about the gender pay gap,
sexualization of children, and the work–life [im]balance. It's not up to
us though to fight their battles for them – they have to do it themselves in their own way. WE will have enough problems fighting the
remnants of public health care in our dotage! (David 2014: 66)

Riding the Wave: Mid-Career Feminists (Cohort Two)?

As we move through the cohorts, the trends seem to shift slightly
and move possibly towards third-wave feminism. This can perhaps
be best summarized by Jocey Quinn, the British feminist who sees
herself as 'riding the waves':

> I consider myself a feminist, many of my beliefs were strongly formed
> through feminist activism in the 80s which I guess may be historically
> second wave but I am alive now and contributing and so *still riding the
> wave I hope* . . . I can see broad distinctions in terms of campaigns about
> violence against women for example where to my mind feminists used
> to hold stronger positions and be more rigorous in seeing connections
> across all aspects of life. Subsequent generations are more global in
> their outlook and in this they are stronger. (David 2014: 66)

Interestingly, the question of where those feminists or women
of colour position themselves in relation to the wave analogy is
yet another perspective, as is evident from Heidi Mirza's trenchant
comments:

> I consider myself a 'third-wave black/postcolonial feminist'. I belong
> to a small but important community of women scholars of colour
> in Britain. There is a generation of postcolonial women who have
> struggled together in academe since the 1970s, and some of us are now

professors! Black British Feminism in the early 1990s was very powerful because it brought together women of colour who were writing
and doing brilliant work but in isolated little 'pockets' in different
universities in the UK. Independently we were writing on similar
themes. Some were just finishing their PhDs, some were already established. Black British Feminism opened up a moment of possibilities
and brought us together to make such a powerful statement. It created
a new subject area based on our collaborative writing. It was such an
energetic and vibrant time. I'm very proud to have been part of this.
(David 2014: 67)

Gemma Moss (now President of BERA) agreed:

I do identify very much as a feminist within the left and TU politics,
though my most active period was as a teacher [my emphasis] . . . I do think
professional third-wave feminism turned feminism into a private language you more or less have to do a doctorate to speak. If feminism
means something then it means something in the real world, not as a
theoretical object in the knowledge-making factory of the academy.
This doesn't mean not holding on to base principles – but I think
something odd has happened to knowledge-making too. So it's a question of sorting out what has really shifted, what stays the same. (David
2014: 67–8)

Among the 'education feminists' most closely associated with
colleagues in the third cohort there was some perplexity as one
said:

Probably yes. There are fewer consensuses about what we are doing.
There are few theoretical or ideological positions that we agree on. So,
diversity and the lack of pride in calling ourselves 'feminist' make for
a diaspora. However, globally we see women rising up and facing up
to their oppressors in the most dramatic and impressive ways. I think
these movements have been possible because of the history of feminism in the West. I think globally feminism is alive, and that locally it
is hidden (gone underground in Vygotsky's sense of the term). (David
2014: 68)

Neatly linking cohorts two and three are the partners Penny Tinkler and Carolyn Jackson: 'We probably would just consider ourselves to be feminists, rather than second-wave feminists, per se. Whilst many of the ideas of second wave feminists have been very influential for both of us, we are uneasy with such distinctions (which can be divisive)' (David 2014: 68).

A Second and a Half Waver

The feminists of the third cohort (i.e., born after 1965) are also questioning of the wave analogy, with some of the younger more international women doubting the uses of the term at all any more, if ever. Those who remain committed to feminism can be seen to be somewhat ambivalent about which cohort they belong to, well articulated by Fin Cullen's comment:

> I think I am probably a second and a half waver. Generationally speaking I should be probably a third waver, but as my early entry into feminism attests the key theoretical thinkers that shaped my baby feminist years were distinctly second wave (and before, I found a copy of Mary Wollstonecraft at sixteen, which opened my eye to the earlier history). However, I did spend some time reading riot grrrl fanzines, and pogoing at riot grrl gigs (see Bikini Kill; Hole; Babes in Toyland) but really I preferred the earlier non-riot grrl and more implicit feminism of the Slits . . . The generation tussles between the 'right' focus and approach that feminism should adopt is intriguing. I think some third wave approaches might be dismissed as not 'beefy' enough. By that I mean that it could be seen to be more concerned with fripperies, and that the deeper questions raised by second wave movement need returning to. (David 2014: 69)

Similarly, Kelly Coate wrote that:

> The theory of course inevitably begins spilling into practice, but discovering feminist politics at the end of the second wave of the

women's movement was like showing up at a party a few days late. Those of us who were young feminists in the early 1990s were caught in between the second and the third wave, trying to figure out in which direction to look. Looking backwards was always done with some envy, through hearing stories of the events that had taken place. My favourite anecdote was about the first women's caucus meeting of the BSA, where the men had to be physically locked out of the room so that they would stop interrupting the women. As it was explained, women's role at the BSA conferences up to that point had largely been one of acknowledging the genius of the men. The idea that the women were finding a room of their own and locking the men out was hugely threatening. We all found out later what happens when men are let back in, which is why we looked back on that history of feminist scholarship with envy and looked forward with some trepidation. (Davis and Evans 2011: 81–2)

Conclusions: Feminism Remains a New Wave of Thinking

While the wave metaphor was heavily debated, all my participants across the three cohorts subscribed to a notion of *feminism*, at very least being about forms of gender equality within society and academe. Many were still working through its meanings for their scholarly work as well as for their political and academic practice. Feminist values transcend specificities of generation, time and place: they suffuse and shine through all three of my cohorts, despite differences of age, location or changing educational, economic and social contexts. A commitment to gender and social justice is a passion for all of my participants in this study, and they have held this dear, across the vicissitudes of their personal, political and professional lives. Nevertheless, there are clear differences in the struggles and achievements of the three cohorts to do with changing socio-political contexts, and the influences of academic or education feminisms on changing and more global neoliberal universities. As we move through the cohorts, as women have entered and stayed within academe, education feminism has changed the universities, although moves to the neoliberal university are now having contradictory, conflicting and paradoxical effects.

Education feminism itself has also changed, both in terms of who is now involved and how they are involved. A most complex issue is the relation between social class and family background and educational or university participation. Feminist origins of working class and lower middle class as 'first-in-the-family' to go to university have increased as HE has expanded. And yet such women, despite this social and geographic mobility, are still constrained and constricted in their reach into the upper echelons of academe: there is still male domination. It is clear how empowering feminism has been for these women's teaching and research, and how important it is for their own academic and personal lives. What is also important is the role that feminism has played in creating a more reflexive and imaginative cross-cutting interdisciplinary approach, especially to being in HE and conducting HE research, as we have seen clearly in the voices of these education feminists (David 2014: 173).

5

Challenging Gender Violence for Children and Young People through Education

Introduction

In this chapter I consider recent feminist research that has contributed to our knowledge and understanding of girls' and boys' lives, and those of men and women, around both violence against women and girls (VAWG) and issues concerning those who are lesbian, gay, bisexual, transgender or queer (LGBTQi). I focus on how education feminists have drawn on the scholarship of those of the early second wave, to tackle not only gender equality but also gender-related violence (GRV). Despite the impressive array of recent feminist scholarship within the field of gender and education, issues around GRV remain marginalized within the corpus of knowledge.

As Alldred and David (2007) noted, this is marginalized in part because of the lack of knowledge and understanding of teachers and others about how to question gender identities, norms and hetero-normativity. Teacher training rarely takes on board these questions, whether as part of pre-service or in-service education or training, focusing more on the neoliberal agenda of educational achievement. As already seen, we found that teachers and health and youth workers do not feel adequately trained, so we set out to provide some initial training to help to develop this. We wanted to embed more gender consciousness in learning at school and/or university and as part of professional practice.

This feminist-activist project combined theoretical and methodological insights from the second wave with the third wave. We started from the position of problematizing the gender binary, as gender normativities can be seen to reflect the broader deconstructive move of third-wave or post-structural feminism and queer theory, in particular. Butler's (1990) articulation of the heterosexual matrix's mutual constitution through the gender binary is a key influence in the project's challenge to hetero-normativity. A broad concept of GRV is compatible with feminist approaches that problematize all inequalities and attend to power differentials across all forms of social difference (race, ethnicity, class, gender, sexual orientation) and with social theory that emphasizes the intersectionality of gender with class and ethnicity (Anthias and Yuval-Davis 1993; Brah 1992).

We developed an innovative approach to gender norms, including machismo and heterosexism, by drawing on two separate strands of activism and theory, namely, work on VAWG around peer relations, sexual abuse or bullying, and anti-homophobia and trans-recognition. A theoretical question for our study was whether it is possible to broaden the focus without undermining an effective intervention on VAWG. As an overall approach, we might favour 'post-identity' frameworks to ensure that essentialisms are not re-inscribed or binaries assumed or the relations between them sustained. So, focusing on these two separate strands, we hoped that we might develop an approach to deal with machismo and heterosexism as gender norms.

The project was designed to allow for four national, or what we called *local*, actions around developing education or training for professionals regarding GRV with children and young people. Our overarching approach and aims were the same, but we allowed for local, contextual differences in method and in specific definition of what constituted an appropriate pilot study at this historic juncture.

Table 5.1 The four local actions in the UK, Ireland, Italy and Spain

Local actions	The training teams	The theoretical orientation
UK (Brunel University, London with UCL IOE)	University researchers with two community or trainer teams: AYP and ROW	GRV: Interpersonal violence, gender norms, peer abuse and risk: safeguarding
Ireland (Maynooth University)	University teachers of youth and community work	GBV: Gender-conscious youth work: personal change
Italy (University of Turin)	University researcher with two local groups: Maurice (LGBTQi) and Demetra (VAWG)	GRV: health and victim support aspects of VAWG and homophobia or abusive forms of LGBT
Spain (University Rovira i Virgili, Tarragona, Catalonia)	University feminist academic's pedagogies with local feminist community groups: Candela (sexualities) and Tamaia (VAWG recovery)	GRV: heteronormativity, 'gender violences' and inclusive environment; personal reflections

The approach that each local action adopted illustrated the differences in the precise terms preferred. As the Irish team explained (Alldred and David 2015: 16), their preference was for the term 'GBV' (gender-based violence), and although the other local actions adopt the term 'GRV', in practice each action problematized homophobia as well as VAWG. Furthermore, employing the same term in *English* might not mean that the situated actions in local contexts and languages have precisely the same definitions and meanings. There are limitations to inter-country comparative studies, and caution must be exercised over comparative conclusions.

A key issue with this study was its inception from a UK perspective and articulation in English, which meant that the specific terms used may not have been as relevant for the other countries, and the comfortable translation of the plural *violencias* into English eludes us (Alldred and David 2015: 16). Indeed, the Spanish team's preference for the plural may distinguish this intervention from other local approaches that use the singular in Spanish. The loose structure of the project was intended to allow the training or educational concept to be rethought in each context.

In what follows, I will present a brief account of the four 'sister' training programmes (one each in Ireland, Italy, Spain and the UK). The different training logics and political interventions they make, as well as the more nuanced differences of social-change projects in particular cultural contexts, deserve individual attention. Overall, we aimed to develop either training or a particular pedagogy, for professionals to work with children and young people at better understanding gender norms and GRV and challenging those norms and practices. We have analysed the actions both qualitatively and quantitatively, but here I present only our qualitative evaluation.

Reflecting on Our Learning from Local Actions

As a result of these four separate but intertwined projects, about 750 practitioners have received training and certification for attendance (across four countries). These trainees have received a ('Cascade') resource to share their learning with their colleagues and new information leaflets are now available on university websites in six countries.

The Irish action developed specialist training for a particular professional group, youth and community workers, through a university education programme, and made a broad intervention by training practitioners already 'in the field'. This team probably produced the most sustainable action because new training is integrated into initial practitioner education at university: it is an impressive legacy.

The UK training had intended to do this, but initial teacher education managers did not accept the offer of free training, even though the same staff had previously delivered smaller elements of it in-house and without certification. Accreditation was difficult to obtain in the time period in the UK but an influential NUT (National Union of Teachers) endorsement was valuable. The UK training was a model of evolving training over successful cohorts and identified lessons about organizational issues that would be important to heed in future.

The Italian action made the biggest intervention among health-sector staff and succeeded in obtaining an external accreditation, which helped attract medical personnel. It also enabled many educational professionals to enhance their understanding, given that studies of gender norms are already included in schools in Italy.

The Spanish action like the Irish, sought personal change and reflexivity about trainees' social positionality and experiences. It perhaps had the strongest claim to measurement of learning or personal impact of the training, having trainer evaluations of learning, trainee self-report, observation and an indicator of learning from the online assessments completed after training.

The Spanish and the UK teams also have information about the interventions the trainees planned to make in their workplaces. The overriding importance of avoiding judgemental attitudes creeping into training, by emphasizing the pedagogy of personal reflexivity, was a challenge. The core approach was one that locates the heterosexist, sexist, racist environment as the problem and understands us all (trainers, trainees and researchers) as produced through our social and specific environments.

Overall, our own learning about how to develop training rather than education, despite using traditional educational contexts, has given us new insights about the difficulties of achieving a good balance between 'hope' and 'despair' when training regarding violence or abuse, especially when a key objective is to increase awareness of these. In particular, we have learnt about the importance of locating GRV in gender inequality and the potential to develop training around GRV or GBV, but perceive the need for theoretical coherence within a training programme. We have also recognized the value of enabling reflection on workplace dynamics and staff experiences, as well as clients' experiences of violence and/or inequality and overall personal and professional development. And we have understood the value of questioning what is identified as violence and what goes unproblematized – both in young people's experiences and in workplace or professional dynamics.

To illustrate these, I now present some of the key features of each of the local 'actions', and our reflections on this process of raising awareness of GRV to develop new understandings and potential future policies. I present a brief snapshot of each country's particular project, followed by some overarching analysis.

The Four Sister 'Feminist Local Actions'

A. The Irish local action

The Irish 'action' was the development of an enhanced equalities training course for youth/community work practitioners in-training (pre-service education), and stand-alone training workshops for youth workers in practice in Ireland. The team included academic teachers and researchers in community and youth work in the Department of Applied Social Studies in Maynooth University. GBV training was delivered primarily to undergraduate and postgraduate students on the community and youth work programmes. These are the initial practitioner formation courses for youth workers. A series of university-based workshops exploring global and local thinking about feminism and its relevance for youth work, and on identifying how gender inequality and violence are addressed in youth work settings and organizations, were hosted, including current discourses on gender among youth workers and young people.

The training delivered to students within the university was provided as part of a larger professional programme of education in which issues relating to equality, diversity and social justice are central. As such, it provided an opportunity both to reassess the position of gender-equality teaching in the current programme content, and to design and deliver new, focused sessions on GBV. The students with whom these focused sessions were delivered were required to contextualize this training in broader

Equality Studies and Professional Practice modules during the year, including their professional practice placements in youth and community organizations. The modules were part of a larger formation programme for equality and social justice.

The conceptual framework for understanding GBV located the root causes of GBV within a continuum of sexism, with unconscious or casual stereotyping at one end and overt gender oppression and violence at the other. It was established within the systemic 'vehicle' of patriarchal society that promotes sexist values and practices at personal, cultural and structural levels. Any form of sexism or gender stereotyping dehumanizes both women and men and violates women. The Irish team preferred the term 'GBV' over 'GRV', to emphasize that this violence is *based* on gender and gender stereotyping, not simply *related* to it.

The project sought to generate further learning for trainees and trainers or educators, building on previous work. The evaluation identified the challenges to implementing learning in practice and gaps in knowledge, skills, tools and resources. An exciting source of insight into their learning was in the written work submitted at the end of training, as well as the individual and small-group presentations to demonstrate understanding and learning.

B. The Italian action

The Italian action, in Turin, was the piloting of a training course called Against Gender-Related Violence: Gender Violence against (and by) Children and Young People: Training for Practitioners. The team included a university researcher based in Turin, and two training partners collaborated with the coordinator to create the training programme, content selection and classroom training activities. One was the Maurice Association on LGBTQi and the other Demetra Support and Listening to Victims of Violence Centre, of the City of Health and Science Agency, of Turin University Hospital.

The Maurice Association was established in 1985 and its aim has always been to fight all types of discrimination and prejudice, with special regard to the right of freedom of expression for one's sexual orientation and gender identity. With headquarters in Turin, it is a member of the LGBT Turin Pride Coordination, a network of associations operating in the Piedmont Region. In 2010, it participated in a project funded by the EU: AHEAD. It has collaborated with the LGBT service of the City of Turin and the province of Turin since 2003, organizing training activities to eliminate all forms of discrimination and prejudice. Its main focus is educational-social.

The Demetra Centre was set up in 2003 and its functions include the provision of healthcare, counselling and support, safe housing and information on public and private sources of help for the victims of violence. The centre works closely with the emergency department of the hospital. It is a member of the city-wide Coordination against VAW, a network of associations that focus on preventing and combating VAW and providing essential relief and support to victims. It has organized training activities since 2004, focusing on VAW in healthcare.

The training was open to professionals who work in contact with children and young people on a daily basis, so as to expand and improve their knowledge and their range of tools, and enable them: first, to better identify and challenge sexist, sexualizing, homophobic, violent or controlling language and behaviours; second, to know when and how to refer children and young people to the most appropriate support services. The new skills acquired by course participants sought to make their workplaces more welcoming and inclusive for children and young people.

Italian partners used the concept of GRV, based on the project definition, of 'sexist, sexualizing or norm-driven bullying and harassment behaviours', with a view to developing an innovative training experience, addressing issues not generally dealt with in training courses on violence and discrimination in Italy. Turin boasts long-standing experience in training on VAWG, and, to a lesser extent, on sexual orientation and gender identity, especially in schools. But these themes are rarely tackled under the same umbrella.

In recent years, even the expressions *violenza di genere* (gender violence) and *violenza maschile* (male violence) are confused in the way the concepts of VAW are used by feminist groups, by mass media, and in local public policies. In particular, 'gender violence' is often used erroneously as a synonym of domestic violence or VAW, clearly showing how 'gender-related issues' are still being reduced to 'the woman question', and how VAW is perceived as a problem that pertains to women alone.

This hampers the process of men taking responsibility and stands in the way of a broader understanding of the phenomenon. On the other hand, many feminists believe that promoting the concept of 'gender violence' – or addressing the issues of discrimination against women and discrimination against LGBTQi people in the same debate – risks concealing or playing down the impact of men's VAW, shifting the attention of public opinion and policy-makers away from the latter.

Fully aware of such concerns, the Turin team worked to combine the knowledge and expertise of trainers coming from two different 'realities' (the Maurice Association with experience in LGBTQi and the Demetra Centre on VAW regarding healthcare), so as to develop a training programme which created a bridge between them.

All the known previous training experiences on violence conducted locally had addressed the issue of *violenza assistita* (violence witnessed) by children. Tackling the theme of violence by and against children and young people in the form of bullying, and especially homo/lesbo/transphobic bullying and cyberbullying, is new. This is notwithstanding the attention paid to the phenomenon of bullying in school, if the treatment of this phenomenon is part of a more comprehensive analysis.

In a project whose ultimate purpose consists of combating violence by and against children and young people, in fact, examining the different types of violence by taking into consideration mutual links and common characteristics is indispensable. Providing tools for critical reflection to professionals who work in contact with children and teenagers, especially those working in the educational sphere, enables them to take action not only in an emergency or to deal with individual cases, but also to create an inclusive climate and to affect the gender paradigm which is the root cause of violent phenomena.

The trainers used a number of expressions ('gender violence', 'violence against children', 'bullying', 'homophobia') related to specific topics addressed, and supplied definitions of various forms of violence. One definition, in particular, was used to analyse the socio-cultural causes of violence, namely, bell hooks' (2004) definition of patriarchal violence, which she suggests is more effective in capturing brutality than 'domestic violence'. It encompasses all types of violence, whether by men or by women who are victims of sexist and patriarchal culture, with its stereotypes and mindset. In this way, the violence that even women sometimes commit against children or, more rarely, against men and other women is in the frame; and its recognition is a step on the road to ending patriarchal culture.

This definition was particularly effective, since it comes close to the concept of GRV: it makes it possible to analyse different types of violence in a coordinated manner, fostering a critical reflection on the causes of violence in our society and the strategies that can be adopted to combat it. The teaching method adopted in the classrooms was mostly interactive. The trainers used a wide range of materials and methods.

The courses were held in the classrooms of Campus Luigi Einaudi of the University of Turin, which provided a 'neutral' space for all participants. The training was open to professionals from social-educational and medical-healthcare areas. Initially, professionals working in the sports field were envisaged as trainees, but due to the limited time and the huge number of applications from the social-educational and medical-healthcare areas (exceeding the programme's capacity), the initiative eventually concentrated on these two only.

The main group of participants were *educators*: first, teachers in kindergarten, primary and secondary school, educational services area of the Municipality of Turin (e.g., toy libraries and youth centres), educators, youth workers, intercultural mediators, social workers and community helpers (municipal service employees, employees and volunteers in cooperatives and associations working in education and social sectors). They were joined by *vigili di prossimità* (neighbourhood police) – the local, community-oriented police who deal with cases of stalking and domestic violence and give training in schools. They are regarded, at least in the way they are perceived in the city, as social operators and not as a coercive force.

The second wave of recruitment was of *health workers:* nurses, paediatric nurses, paediatricians, family doctors, hospital doctors, psychologists, psychiatrists and some female students from the degree course on paediatric nursing, all of whom were employees of public organizations. Other participants included civil servants and politicians who did not work with children/young people directly, but wanted to participate in order to implement anti-gender violence policies in their spheres, or to propose awareness-raising activities in their companies/organizations.

Over 210 people enrolled on the training courses: only fourteen participants (less than 17 per cent) were men. This tiny representation of men illustrates one of the problems of tackling GRV, that when attendance at a course is voluntary, GRV attracts more interest or commitment from women. Over a third of the attendees had never participated in training programmes on GRV themes. Two out of five had received some training on a few of the concerns addressed, while 20 per cent had previously undertaken courses relevant to all aspects.

C. The Spanish local action

The Spanish training, in Catalonia, was called Youth, Gender and Violence: Gaining Agency in Prevention, and consisted of training sessions, a virtual tutorial (using an online platform of the virtual campus at University Roviri i Virgili (URV)) and feedback. Research suggests that there are high levels of all types of gender violence (between couples, social violence, LGBT violence) among young people in Spain (Biglia, Olivella-Quintana and Jimenez-Perez 2013). But young people are poor at detecting gender discrimination (Alberdi, Escario and Matas 2000; Biglia and Luna 2012; Biglia and Velasco 2012) and envisage primarily legal solutions (Carvajal and Vázquez 2009).

In the Catalan training, a wide definition of GRV was adopted by the team, expressed with the Spanish term of *violencias de género* (gender violences) (Biglia and San Marti 2007). This is to make clear that gender itself is a form of violence because it forces people to fit into a predefined, dichotomous (or binary) construction of identity. Therefore gender violences are all the forms of violence that are exercised and/or reproduced in gender relations and social roles. The sex or gender of the subject that exercises or receives the violence/s is therefore irrelevant as even an ungendered body or institution can exercise it. The interconnection between the construction of gender and the heterosexual imperative means that violence against people who are LGBT is also understood as an expression of gender violences.

The focus is on a wide understanding of violence that includes, amongst other things, power exercised in relationships, lesbo/ homo/transphobia, and violence enacted through institutional, symbolic and community relations. However, if different forms of gender violence share their roots, they are not equivalent and they did not necessarily produce the same material and emotional effects. Hence it is important to know their cause, process and, in particular, their effect. An intersectional approach is essential because gender violences have to be understood in the context of the embodied subject experiencing it in a specific socio-cultural context.

The idea was to design an innovative course to show that gender violences are not a personal problem between two subjects (often assumed to be a male and a female one) but have structural, hetero-patriarchal roots. This should help professionals who work with young people make interventions that are respectful of difference. Following feminist perspectives, the training not only focused on theoretical concepts, but also involved personal questioning of the internalization and reproduction of gender stereotypes as trainees linked the curriculum to their own lives (Giraldo and Colyar 2012). The course aimed to produce a critical consciousness and promote awareness and commitment amongst those who attended as active agents in transformation of social norms. Hence it was designed as a personal and collective journey for participants, and as a political intervention to produce social change (Mayberry 2001). Following Campbell (2002), the team's own political commitments led to 'collaborative, experiential, egalitarian, interactive and empowering processes that connect rational, relational and affective dimensions facilitating cooperative learning' (Luxán, Serrano and Biglia 2011: 156).

The training was informed by Tisdell's (1998) postmodern feminist pedagogy: first, to show that knowledge is socially constructed and there is no single reality; second, to create spaces where participants can use their own voice and recognize that silence does not mean lack of agency; third, to recognize that power relations will rise up in each teaching–learning space, and to allow the questioning of sources of authority; fourth, to make intersectionality and situatedness explicit and work with participants' specific positionalities; fifth, to include emancipatory activities at participant and community level.

The two partner feminist associations, Candela and Tamaia, delivered the training. Candela is a non-profit organization that, since 2004, has worked to promote feminist social transformation from a community perspective, based on cooperation and mutual support. Candela works in the areas of the prevention of GRV by delivering comprehensive education on sexualities. Tamaia is a pioneer organization that has worked on VAW since 1992. It developed a conceptual framework for understanding VAW and a specialized intervention and recovery programme for women. Its team of professionals has expertise in violence intervention, prevention and training.

The Spanish team exchanged views on gender violences over a considerable time to develop the training focus and pedagogy. A concern was that the different cultural backgrounds and perspectives of the training partners might result in an incoherent training programme, allowing trainees to remain convinced that violence in couple relationships and violence against LGTB people are two completely different problems.

The Department of Education (DE) of the Catalonian government, responsible for education policy in the region, recruited the trainees to the initial courses. The Catalan Youth Agency (ACJ), a public body linked to the Department of Youth of the Catalan government, which provides services for young people, recruited trainees for the second round. The plan was to deliver all training in Barcelona, but the ACJ explained the greater need for training in smaller Catalan cities (Girona, Lleida, Manresa and Cambrills) because there are fewer GRV training opportunities. The DE recognized the training as professional development, so the course was recognized for national employment applications for teachers and other professionals. Nonetheless, only two participants reported that the certificate was their primary reason for enrolment.

Two hundred people were recruited for the training, the majority of whom were women (84 per cent), and born in Catalonia. They had high levels of education (56 per cent undergraduate degrees, 35 per cent master's or PhD levels); the average age was 40.5 years. Participants were quite homogeneous (female, well educated and non-migrant) and fairly representative of professionals in this region. Many of them (61 per cent) had already attended some training on GRV and a small group (6 per cent) had completed a Masters course or specialist training on GRV.

It is important to note that, in the initial survey, two thirds of participants stated that their main motivation for enrolling was to develop tools and skills to use at work. Three-quarters of teachers had this aim. Almost half of all participants stated that their main expectation was to acquire tools useful at work, and a third aimed at developing strategies to address the problem of gender-related violences.

The Spanish law against GRV (Organic Law 1/2004) includes eleven Articles of preventative measures, several of which are educational. Catalan law regarding *machista* violence (Law 5/2008) also includes preventative measures, including educational ones, but there appear to be no plans for evaluating their effectiveness.

The evaluation of a sensitive topic such as this needs to be extremely careful and assume a feminist perspective, such as in a feminist-activist research process (Biglia 2007) that is committed to social transformation and sensitive to participants' different views (Haraway 1997). Accordingly, we believe that many elements have to be considered to evaluate the strength and limitations of pedagogical design. In this sense, the learning of the participants is an important element but other factors, such as their satisfaction with the project or the coherence with a feminist pedagogical perspective, are also extremely relevant.

For this reason, a mixed-method research design was used, giving importance to the personal experiences and meaning of participants (both trainees and trainers) but also including the external evaluators' (the researchers') points of view.

D. The UK local action

The UK's local action was a training course on GRV, delivered in England, with a different trainer and focus each day, about both gender inequalities and LGBTQi. It deconstructed 'gender', identified inequality and violence within the workplace as well as elsewhere in the lives of young people, and explained the law and legal remedies and how to discuss positive relationships with young people. It also directed the focus of trainees on to the actions that they planned to undertake in their workplaces. Researchers in the Centre for Youth Work Studies at Brunel University, London, coordinated the training that emerged, given the difficulties in finding appropriate recruits or participants. It also was delivered as a partnership with two key distinctive partners: About Young People (AYP) and Rights of Women (ROW).

Youth and community workers founded AYP about fifteen years ago, to work with young people in local settings. ROW was established as a second-wave feminist legal organization in the 1970s. It has continued to campaign and argue for women's rights consistently, providing a critique of emerging legislation. Due to challenges in participant recruitment, a decision was made to diversify delivery sites, which brought in two university sites. The training was largely delivered and coordinated by university staff, but not based within university courses as in the case of the Irish local action.

Training was delivered over a period to allow time for learning to be embedded in the practice of the participants. During the first phase (planning and participant recruitment), it was decided that the programme would focus on achieving the following overall aims and outcomes, which were based on the overall project aims, namely, to enable youth practitioners to: (a) recognize GRV in their settings; (b) intervene confidently and take action to combat GRV; (c) refer to appropriate agencies; and (d) pass on their learning to colleagues.

The UK team adopted a broad definition of GRV in line with the definition set by the project, and identified three themes within it: namely, VAW and children (not only girls); violence based on homophobia and transphobia; violence based on 'machismo' (which might include violence from men with hegemonic masculinities towards other men). The approach to the topic and training agreed among the team was that: violence was understood in the context of and produced by inequality; intersectionality was important to all, such that racial- and age-based inequalities in particular were kept in view; structural and cultural levels of analysis were brought to the understanding of problematic behaviour, rather than individualizing (psychological or criminological) approaches; and a critical gaze was applied to workplace relationships, as well as to relationships among young people.

Depersonalizing techniques were used, and trainees were not asked to reflect on their own experience because it was a one-off event so lacked ongoing support, and because some cohorts had colleagues training alongside each other or student peers. Disclosure was actively discouraged, but positive approaches to working with young people – constructive ways of helping young people identify their relationship hopes and preferences – were encouraged, informed by youth-work pedagogies that prioritized supporting young people to reach their own conclusions. On the other hand, health-promotion techniques were also used, which sought to convince participants of predetermined positive messages.

We recognized that different parties might be informed by a range of approaches to GRV. Theoretical approaches used to help trainees problematized dynamics that they had taken for granted previously. It was agreed by all trainers that narrowing or expanding the themes within GRV depended on what was identified as an individual, institutional, community or professional need for each cohort (training group) of participants. This approach allowed the training team to respond to the issues raised in the sessions and at recruitment stage by gatekeepers (e.g., service or training managers). Additionally, we asked a question at the registration stage about themes practitioners were interested in exploring. Sexual exploitation and female genital mutilation (FGM) were identified as key themes for training, highlighting the importance of including these to gain credibility for the training amongst senior managers who allowed teams to attend training.

Two themes that came up repeatedly were sexual violence targeted by gang members against young girls associated with other gangs, and sexual violence being used to control gang identities. Another key theme was the issue of working with faith communities. Some of the critique from participants was that the training was 'too white and too secular', in other words not intersectional enough. In addition to the needs of the trainees, the 'needs' of the trainers were a factor in selecting the themes that were addressed under the GRV definition. For example, the research and practice expertise (or comfort zones) of AYP dictated the more in-depth focus on violence and less detailed analysis of gender.

Moreover, ROW, as a feminist organization based on the principles of second-wave feminism, reiterated their need to focus primarily on the legal aspects of VAW. This sometimes led to a 'hierarchy of themes', with VAWG at the top and general machismo at the bottom. In order to counter this, a trainer from a health-promotion background built in a series of activities that addressed 'promoting healthy relationships' with young people. For ROW, there was the added difficulty of hetero-normativity being built into the British legal system, which made it seem that the trainers were being hetero-normative and uncritical. They remedied this by developing some new case studies of same-sex relationships. All of this meant that there was sometimes a theoretical difference and potential incongruence regarding the language used between individual trainers to contextualize GRV, and this was highly political. Although this did not have a negative impact on the training, further research might explore the need for theoretical congruence in training, or whether it is manageable to learn from sessions embodying different perspectives.

There were about 200 participants overall. The majority worked in professional roles as community, youth or social workers, while a very small proportion (16 per cent), mainly women, were teachers. The vast majority were also experienced professionals, but few had received any GRV training previously (13 per cent). The initial target audiences for the training were teachers in training and youth workers already in practice (although not necessarily established practitioners), alongside a small number of allied professionals. As initial take-up amongst the target group (particularly trainee teachers) was low, we made the decision to switch from initial teacher education to youth-worker training.

Interestingly, the largest cohorts of participants were from Coventry, which led the training team to conclude that the 'need' was more pressing outside of London where practitioners suffer from 'opportunity fatigue'. The programme was created as a basic introduction for those who would be dealing with homophobic/sexist bullying in the playground or youth club. However, those who signed up already had a good basic knowledge and had been on previous training, which included university-based professional education. Moreover, participants were already quite established in their professional roles. The broader intake of professionals also meant that we made a conscious decision to leave the training as open to change as possible.

From the point of view of the trainers, this seemed to work well. A trainer from AYP commented that the overall programme appeared to have been very well received by the majority of practitioners. Although mixed professional groups can present challenges, on the whole it appears to make for more productive discussions, as practitioners are required to explore their own practice settings with others who may be less familiar with these settings. Participants also highlighted the benefits of learning in an inter-professional environment. Many noted in their evaluations that they enjoyed learning from the variety of expertise and professions. It is the view of the training and research team that this unintended outcome added real value to the UK programme (Alldred and David 2015: 49).

Diversity in Evaluations of the Local Actions

We conducted evaluations of the training actions from the points of view of both the trainees and the trainers, and from the point of view of the research. We focused upon personal, professional and trainer evaluations, and then on our overall lessons from the project as a whole. Some of the key comments from the individual local actions are as follows, illustrating its rich diversity.

First, **the Irish team** argued that:

> We also learned that the sexism being promoted through social media, which is targeted particularly at young people, is considerably more intense than what is currently available through public broadcasting media (targeted primarily at adults). Participants provided examples of 'children's' games where, in order to progress to the next level of the game, 'players' are invited in one example to kill prostitutes, and to kill babies in another example. Participants constantly expressed concern about the power social media has in the socialization of young people insofar as the values conveyed are 'communicated' personally and often privately, relatively unmediated by adults who can, in other arenas, monitor, advise or raise questions with young people about these influential sources of information . . .
>
> There was a sense that challenging sexualized images of women, or the sexualizing and controlling language and behaviour of men, would display a sort of 'prudishness' that could 'put young people off'. Participants often noticed their discomfort with young women's explicitly sexualized self-expression, experiencing confusion about whether this is indicative of liberation or oppression. While it seems sexism – the stereotyped expectations of women's work, domestic and social roles and responsibilities – has shifted, and the roles previously

held as cultural norms appear to have been somewhat dismantled, the sexualization of women has exponentially expanded under the guise of 'liberation' (Thomas 2003). (Alldred and David 2015: 52)

Consequently, there have also been defensive reactions to the information from some women participants, insisting that their gender-stereotyped behaviour is chosen freely and that they do not find it oppressive (Alldred and David 2015: 52). The pervasiveness of sexism came to participants' attention, and this time within their own youth-work context. They noted that they had not considered this as gender stereotyping before: for example, 'We automatically offer sports activities to boys and cooking to girls, and the young people automatically accept that.' There was also a dawning awareness of gendered stereotyping in the allocation of youth workers' roles and responsibilities (whether or not the manager was male or female). Overall, it was recognized that the design and evaluation of youth work needs to be considered through a gender lens, and more needs to be put in place to support workers continuously to challenge sexism in the work arena, and to work directly with young people on raising their awareness and informing their choices.

Second, **in Italy**, many participants stressed the fact that they had found the training interesting and stimulating and they felt enriched by it, especially because it tackled aspects that were new even to people who had participated in other training on GRV themes, such as the LGBT community, and because of the links indicated between violence and health consequences, such as eating disorders. They appreciated the attention paid to verbal and psychological violence. Symbolic violence and verbal abuse were recognized as normalized and hence more insidious and more difficult to counter, and this is precisely the reason why it is important to scrutinize these types of violence. Participants' acquisition of knowledge about the network of services available in the region was valued highly as an important tool assisting them to know where, how and to whom cases of violence should be referred, and who to consult about doubts and questions when coming across a situation of violence or suspected violence.

It reminded participants that they were part of a network and system, not going it alone to tackle violence, and so was significant psychologically/emotionally, as well as practically. So, when a participant stated, 'In the sense that if confusion was one of the aims of the training, well then, we succeeded,' this seemingly negative statement actually expressed precisely the need described above, and fulfilled one of the objectives of the trainers: that participants left the training with more questions, more doubts. The training could not leave trainees feeling *fully* prepared, but perhaps more importantly left participants expressing a desire to go on studying these issues, attend other courses, and bring these themes to their workplaces in order to share resources and repeat similar training activities.

Even when professionals are willing and able to broach issues of sexuality and sexual identity, the methods and tools at hand are woefully stereotypical or hetero-normative, as some participants such as one sex-education secondary teacher reflected. Only after the training, and after she had reflected on how she might sometimes manage to raise awareness of same-sex attraction while failing to shift young people's conviction that homosexuality 'is not natural', did this woman come to recognize how she was simultaneously upholding heterosexuality as the norm by having no single-sex couples depicted in the teaching resources. This highlighted the need for an open approach, but also the need for new modalities and criticalities in teaching and teaching materials (Alldred and David 2015: 58).

Third, **the Spanish team** concluded that the collaborative design work between training partners and researchers was successful. A trainee said: 'One of the best [trainings] I've ever done for coherence between sessions, methodology, materials and the relations between professionals.' The reflexive methodology and activities that prompted participants to start from their own feelings/experience probably contributed to high scores for the internalization of topics, self-empowerment and knowledge retention.

Many participants spoke positively about personal changes produced by the course, for example:

The course makes me conscious of many topics related to GRV, previously unnoticed. I think the best thing about this course is exactly that: if we, professionals in contact with young people, are clear about these situations, we can develop strategies to face them or at least, ways of sending equalities messages to more marginalized groups . . . I think that it allows me to see machismo as a deep scar in society, and how even people like me, who are sensitized to the topic and have tried to change it, have hidden points. (Alldred and David 2015: 60)

Trainees experienced a great improvement in their capacity to identify gender norms and expectations, which probably relates to the innovative focus on the significance of hetero-normativity in the construction of gender. Satisfaction with specific aspects of the training is not always homogeneous – for example, teachers and youth workers rated trainers' knowledge more highly than did other professionals (especially nurses). This is consistent with the higher satisfaction of teachers with the respect for personal rhythms of work and for networking in the training (both aspects less valued by nurses). Trainers viewed teachers as most able to share their professional experiences, doubts, difficulties and fears. This could be because they were more comfortable with the training pedagogy and more used to working from their own experience. Teachers and youth officers appreciated the ability of trainers to make sessions dynamic. However, in the view of the trainers and researchers and from analysing the actions implemented, the theoretical parts were crucial elements in the training. The groups that seemed to work best were those including participants with more advanced prior training on GRV, and for these the dynamic was fast and fluid and debates were more in-depth.

Finally, given the diversity of **the UK's training**, it is best to consider testimonials from some of the participants:

'I felt that more/all staff need this training to make sure that children have an opportunity to talk to someone openly. Today deepened and refreshed my existing knowledge of the issue of GRV.'

'I now have a better understanding of GRV, and how it can take place no matter where you are.'

'I have a better understanding of where GRV is relevant to my practice and common areas to be aware of.'

'I now understand the difference between gender and sex and how we constantly reinforce ideologies/stereotypes unconsciously as we do it to a certain extent with YP to build relationships.'

'I learnt how to break down GRV into what we [are] tolerating and not tolerating. I can now proactively challenge this framework.'

'I will share the information from today with my staff (training) and help YP think about good/healthy/happy relationships and sex.'

'What a healthy relationship should be like, how to recognize inappropriate behaviour, laws/legislation regarding sexual acts/consent.'

'I learnt about organizations which I can refer colleagues, students, parents to and resources to refer colleagues, students, and parents to.' (Alldred and David 2015: 64)

Reflections on the Feminist Research Focus on GRV and VAWG

Overall, the four different actions led us to acknowledge that there is a real and substantive interest and need to address issues related to gender, identity and equality. First, we were alerted to how pervasive and 'normal' GBV is in Ireland today. Participants recognized their role, responsibility and potential effectiveness in addressing issues of GBV, particularly with young women and young people who identify as LGBTQ, who are struggling with and trying to challenge gender oppression. Youth workers have a specially privileged role in the social development of young people, able to witness and create opportunities for young people to socialize, and young people confide in youth workers about intimate issues in a way they do not with other professionals or even family members (National Youth Council of Ireland 2014).

Providing specific training on GBV for youth workers is vital if they are to meet the obligations of their contact with young people. Therefore, youth workers need training that provides opportunities to examine and explore their own personal and cultural, hidden, assumptions about gender norms and values, and the current forces of socialization on young people along with the content of the messages they convey. Youth workers need opportunities to develop practice skills for making interventions with young people – including spontaneously challenging young people's behaviour and designing and developing planned programmes – and to monitor organizational policies and practices that will combat GBV.

Exploring personal experience is intense and intimate work. Participants need to be forewarned that this work can be emotionally challenging (Alldred and David 2015: 83). Participants reported that separate-sex groups 'felt safer' and they found it 'easier to discuss' issues when they were in all-female or all-male groups. Also, in each cohort of students there was at least one student who had experienced severe abuse in their immediate social group or family. Trainers need to be prepared and skilled at responding to and supporting both the participants who disclose these experiences and others who are in the group.

Consistently, male participants found it difficult not to feel 'blamed' or to become defensive in the initial stages of discussions. Gay men said that while they could understand the benefits and importance of being in all-female or all-male groups, they found it uncomfortable discussing sexism in an all-male group. This can provide for important discussions on the dominance of heteronormative culture and the 'might-is-right' message inherent in male stereotyping that leads to the use of violence. However, forming separate-sex groups can also impact negatively or become intensely uncomfortable, especially for those who identify as transgender or who do not want to identify their orientation publicly. This personal work is necessary for and has a strong impact on youth workers, who are role models for young people and therefore must be gender-conscious practitioners, despite all its challenges.

Exploring the socialization of young people provided clear insights into the sexism being promoted through social media, which are targeted particularly at young people and is considerably more intense than what is currently available through public broadcasting and media targeted primarily at adults. The values conveyed through social media are communicated to young people personally and privately, and this is relatively unmediated by adults who can, in other arenas, monitor, advise or raise questions with young people about these influential sources of information. Consequently, youth workers and those who train them need to become more 'literate' in social media, to develop skills to identify, intervene in and challenge sexism and GBV in this relatively new public-private space that perpetuates it. Related to this is the need to raise awareness of the link between the sexual liberation of women and its confusion with the sexualization of women.

Participants often noticed their own discomfort with young women's explicitly sexualized self-expression, and confusion about whether this is a liberation or part of the oppression. Opportunities for debate and discussion on this area of gender expression proved to be rich, learning about how GBV can be 'packaged and sold' as acceptable. At the systemic or structural level, the intersectionality of sexism, homophobia and racism provided a useful analytical tool for understanding how GBV becomes 'normalized', and the fact that doing nothing perpetuates it. When considered within the context of human rights, the role and impact of culture and religion/religious-based values in the perpetuation of sexism helped to 'secularize' discussions without fear of racism. Participants recognised that they were constrained by social structures, yet capable of acting as agents within and upon them. This recognition enabled them to deepen their understanding of the unconscious collusion with sexism of well-meaning men and women and to strengthen their commitment to addressing GBV.

Participants noted the need to name sexism and gender as a core theme for youth-work practice and specifically at organizational and sectoral policy level. Youth work and community work need to be evaluated and monitored using a gender lens. This involves practitioners consistently disaggregating measures of inputs and outcomes of their work for young women and young men.

Finally, once participants began to appreciate the pervasiveness of sexism and GBV, there was often a sense of being overwhelmed. This was combated when the training moved to identifying concrete ways that practitioners can intervene in, interrupt and combat sexism in their everyday lives and work. It was noted how little work is being undertaken in youth-work contexts on gender roles and masculinity with young men, or with young women on their experience as young *women*, rather than their experience of being young people. It was noted that there was little being done on developing respectful, healthy relationships (outside of sex-education programmes where it is dealt with in a small way). Further, many practitioners were unaware of where to get programme materials.

Similarly, the Italian action noted that LGBTQi community-related themes continue to be the most ignored. In this training experience, thanks to the concept of GRV, it proved possible to tackle such themes, providing stimulus and engendering reflection. Starting from an analysis of the construction of sexual identity in our society, and challenging the binary, hetero-normative and heterosexist vision of gender, proved to be a valuable method, which supplied new understandings and terminology. It also paved the way for a broader reflection on the various types of GRV and the invisibility of such violence as a result of hetero-normativity. It was important to have the participants explore the cultural roots of violence, and the violence built into the language, even before behaviour.

At the same time, it was essential to provide effective anti-violence tools for everyday use. Of these, the local network is surely the most important: it is not sufficient to supply information on existing services. The fact that the trainers, through their services, were part of the city network definitely helped: the participants were able to exchange views with professionals who, besides being trainers, work on a daily basis within the network and therefore could refer to the workings of the network with concrete examples and cases. Their willingness to help enabled participants to begin using the network from the start, asking for advice on actual cases and beginning to move between the different services.

In a city like Turin, where services are numerous, merely offering a list of services would be disorienting; instead, people need teaching how to begin moving in the network. Training for professionals on GRV should make use of interactive methods, providing ample time for exchanges between trainers and trainees, and among trainees. To this end, it is essential to create a favourable climate in the class, starting with the 'classroom agreement'. Trainers need to keep reminding people that there are no ready-made solutions or remedies that apply to all situations: there are tools that we can use, keeping in mind that each case will be different. The novelty and criticality of the topic highlighted the need for new modalities and criticalities in teaching and new teaching materials. The students expressed a desire to study gender- and violence-related issues within the framework of their university degree courses.

In Spain, it was concluded that: 'The course has been most influential in improving [participants'] sensitivity; in the identification of categories of violence . . . in challenging false beliefs, and motivating a need for change. Now we have conscientious professionals motivated to intervene, and this is a great outcome of the training process.' Many participants felt that they had learnt a lot on the course, especially in relation to LGBTQi GRV and in their confidence about interventions. They were also very satisfied with the exercises undertaken and the resources provided, so we imagine that they have been empowered in the process and gained greater awareness of GRV.

However, as Colás and Jiménez (2006) have argued, awareness does not automatically produce appropriate actions; critical awareness may be the prerequisite, in order to comprehend a situation and to transform it. But, as Bondi (2009) has commented, it is not easy to teach reflexivity, and ongoing personal and collective work is needed in order to learn how to apply knowledge in practice. Following the suggestions of Cook-Sather (2007), and coherent with a feminist pedagogy, we have tried to create opportunities for participants to gain critical distance from their experiences and then to analyse them. This process is time-consuming, and participants on the training recognized that. Indeed, an increase in the length of the course was consistently requested. The trainers and researcher were also pleased with the outcomes from the course, and the positive feedback given by most participants.

We would also note the importance of reflection and self-awareness on the part of trainers, to encourage continuous improvement in training. As a consequence of developments in pedagogical design, trainers reported more confidence and consequently feeling more comfortable and therefore flexible in the sessions. Good-quality trainers possessing expertise and experience in the course topic are essential. However, it is important to note that the materials developed by trainers in the project would need to be adapted for use by others in the future. Recognizing situatedness and the effects of intersectionality, we must acknowledge that pedagogical material cannot necessarily be used in the same form in different contexts or by different trainers. However, some materials (for example, the online PowerPoint presentation and the Cascade resource material) can be good starting points for expert trainers to organize their own courses.

Further research and interventions are needed first, around the issue of participants and trainers confronting their own sexist, racist or homophobic prejudices. As one trainer noted of participants: 'We have been able to influence how they intervene, but not enough to make them adopt an intercultural perspective. This is a general need not always recognized.' Apart from these specific issues, we would also note the importance of reflection and self-awareness on the part of trainers, to encourage continuous improvement in training.

Second, we note the difficulty of designing the course dynamics to make participants aware of the effect of intersectionality in GRV. This was due in part to this issue being addressed only on a theoretical level, and in part to the homogeneity of our participants. When, in one group, two participants were openly trans, it was easier to facilitate a debate on gender violences that was not simply abstract. This discussion was not focused directly on the trans people's experiences, but their presence made other participants connect with their own experience of normativity in gender practices. We believe that a greater focus on intersectionality in

GRV training is extremely important, and deserves more specific research.

The UK analysis demonstrates that the training outcomes of the UK programme were met from the point of view of the participants. They left feeling that they had gained new knowledge, understanding and skills to tackle the themes of GRV explored in the training, and the legal aspect, in particular, was the most useful for them. Additionally, we can see from the action plans that the seeds have been planted for our participants to make initial interventions to tackle GRV with and amongst the young people they work with, and within the organizations in which they are located. There was a high level of planned activity as a result of training. Each type of professional at each level had a meaningful action the training had put them in mind of and all identified that organizational change was needed. Saying this, the current data set does not allow us to draw conclusions on whether the new knowledge and understanding of GRV as an effect of power inequalities has been embedded as praxis among our participants.

Both trainers and researchers were concerned that the concept of GRV was being translated differently, depending upon philosophical problems and professional experiences of both trainers and participants. Further analysis is needed that explains how actions were discursively constructed, and if we achieved legibility in the work context. In addition, the training perhaps underestimated the role that location/space and positionality played. For example, for those in faith-based work settings, there was a complexity of taking 'secular' feminism/critical pedagogy to (often heterosexual male) communal leaders from an orthodox faith resistant to some of the themes within GRV. These participants need more intensive support to navigate a path to embed the training in their practice. Moreover, it is yet to be determined if a feminist or critical praxis can be achieved from attending a short burst of continuing professional development. This is evident by participants highlighting that making the changes needed to tackle GRV required managerial and strategic-level input. It was noticeable to many that very few senior managers attended the training.

In addition, the group observations highlighted that there was a level of anxiety about being supported by organizations or institutions and the impact that professional 'audit' cultures have on attempting to form a critical praxis. For example, some trainee teachers highlighted the shortened school day and narrowing of curriculum as an obstacle to embedding the training in practice. Others highlighted lack of resources in the voluntary sector where much youth work is now delivered. One of the trainers, who is also an experienced youth worker, raised concerns that 'Pandora's box' had been opened and that participants needed supervision and development support for learning to be meaningful.

Conclusions: Learning from an Education Feminist Project

While the GAP work project had a complex structure, it has enabled us, as activist-feminist researchers, to study how to develop education to facilitate greater understanding of GRV and VAWG amongst and by children and young people. Given that we were working with researchers in four very different socio-political and cultural contexts, and yet broadly sharing a theoretical perspective on gender inequalities and GRV, we were made critically aware of the immense need to problematize everyday social norms and to raise awareness of 'gender violences' and the violence 'of gender'. There is a need to de-individualize by recognizing the power relations that structure societies, albeit differently and to differing effects for individuals. Centring a multinational project in a country or language sets up particular dynamics within the group and also conceptually and politically. Research and professional practice need to be in dialogue with activists and those focused on social justice goals, in order not to limit aspirations for change or to focus exclusively on the negative.

Comprehensive legislation on GRV that also recognizes the specificity of young people and adopts an intersectional approach is urgently needed to support situated and effective interventions against GRV. Legislation and social policies are a hugely important contextual element and it is important for youth and educational practitioners to be informed about the law. This can empower them to adopt a bold stance because they are confident of legal boundaries. Intervening to tackle GRV and the values that sustain it is a broad aim that needs not only to mobilize professionals in everyday contact with children and young people, but to create widespread and profound social change. Amongst professionals, there is a gaping need and hunger for training on GRV (however it is framed), and for ongoing support to improve professional practice. There may also be a specific need for the training of men by male professionals to deal with their own feelings (Daniels 2012). It is also important that practitioners are reflexive about the account of the problem embedded in their work practices and approaches.

Finally, further and longer-term research is needed to study the efficacy of training to improve professional practice in supporting and referring young people facing violence, and intervening to tackle violence. It is clear that at present there is a lack of commitment and preparedness of schools, at least in the UK and Ireland, to undertake GRV prevention work. The lack of opportunity and time given by schools to enable education professionals to participate in training was one of the most significant challenges to developing strong interventions.

The GAP project examined what can be done around training and best practice across four European countries, demonstrating it is possible to develop innovative training that has an impact on participants. Yet this can only be the first step in a much longer process of getting countries, local areas, organizations and communities working with young people to tackle the unacceptably high levels of GRV. This is to raise personal awareness of the embeddedness of gender inequality in our own everyday practices, including how these are reinforced through our interactions with others. Understanding GRV as a continuum as originally developed by the feminist Liz Kelly (1988) is helpful. We need to develop an understanding of how discursive, affective and material structures reinforce gender inequality, in turn driving GRV. The theoretical frameworks of post-structuralism and intersectionality are most productive for understanding societal structures and how everyday practices are shaped by and, in turn, reproduce these, while at the same time emphasizing there is always the potential to unsettle these structures, especially through sensitive education.

6

Reflections on a Feminist Educational Manifesto

Introduction

In this concluding chapter, I review the complex argument that I have made about the histories of feminism, the women's liberation movement (WLM) and the struggles for women's socio-legal rights, as part of so-called 'global feminism' and gender equality in education in changing international socio-economic and political contexts. In particular, I reiterate how we, as feminists, have achieved a great deal in terms of our thinking, knowledge, learning and insights. We are wise to the struggles over knowledge and learning, but also, feminism, as we have seen, is clearly on the global political agenda: as women's rights. The kinds of feminism that I have been arguing for, however, go beyond women's rights and women's equality – beyond the 'numbers game'.

Nevertheless, we should celebrate the fact that our arguments are on the global agenda and, to some extent, taken seriously. But gender equality cannot have been achieved, if violence against women and girls (VAWG) and gender-related violence (GRV) remain unresolved questions. What kind of equality have we achieved if women and girls, along with young boys, remain subject to sexual abuse and harassment, bullying, rape and violence?

A report from the End Violence Against Women coalition, UK (EVAW) found that services in the UK for abuse victims are struggling because of 'frontline failings' and more than 100 women a year are still killed by a current or former partner (Townsend 2015). Another report from the EU Agency for Fundamental Rights found that 'about a third of all women in the EU have experienced either physical or sexual violence since the age of 15' (2014: 167). As Morley (2013) argued, this is 'misogyny masquerading as metrics'. How do we go beyond the numbers game and 'change the rules of the neo-patriarchal game'?

I also discuss what we have learnt from these struggles to build upon our learning and particular feminist pedagogies, despite the contestation. I revisit my argument about the learning from waves of feminism, and how empowering feminist education has been across the generations. New waves of feminism, in the twenty-first century, are building on this heritage, developing exciting new strategies for formal and informal ways of learning, and new pedagogies that might better counter neoliberalism and its reincorporation of neo-patriarchy in forms of individualism (Renold, Ringrose and Egan 2015).

Building upon feminist gains in wisdom and insights, I re-envision the idea of 'demands' of the WLM of the 1970s, or 'from cradle to grave' to put it back in terms of the agenda for the British welfare state, almost seventy years ago now. Given the huge socio-economic and political transformations, is it possible to think through what elements of these demands could usefully be reinvoked as part of a feminist manifesto today? In particular, how can we relate those 'demands on the social democratic state' to demands on the reconfigured neoliberal, neo-patriarchal state and dealing with the seventh demand in particular: elimination of VAWG?

This neoliberal state is both much less interventionist fifty years on, and also far more committed to rampant individualism and market competition (Campbell 2013; Fraser 2013). It has found various ways of infiltrating across new media and informal education, especially in and through sexualization. Can our demands be adapted to new forms of democratization for new generations and waves of not only feminists but also children and young people? What precisely would that entail for forms of education? How can we think about dignity and respect for future generations as well as equality and fairness, to ensure that all are safeguarded from risks of GRV?

Any programme of change would need to tackle these questions of VAWG and GRV through a systematic form of lifelong learning, through families, communities, schools and higher education (HE). A radically new social philosophy or sociological approach is needed towards what it means to be fully human, regardless of one's gender or sexuality. The evidence about gender and sexualities, and their conscious and unconscious effects within and beyond schooling, have become critical to feminist social-scientific and psycho-social studies. They are ways of thinking about a new gender consciousness that is subtler than a critique of gender norms or normativity per se, also addressing social and mental well-being. How can we ensure that feminist ideas and knowledge are used to further this?

As the GAP work project has shown, we need an adequate and intricate programme of teacher and youth professional education or training that makes explicit gender consciousness and the social conditions of gender. This programme needs to focus on everyday sexism and everyday violence, and their embeddedness in our everyday lives, to deal with other questions of GRV. This entails considering waves of feminist strategies or activism both through academia and more widely as grassroots or street politics. It also means going beyond what are seen as current political and economic realities and acceptance of the inevitability of gender power and politics in this current juncture of neoliberalism, with its overarching emphasis on austerity as the way to a better world.

The resurgence of feminism not only in academia but amongst new generations in the twenty-first century in politics, including social media, gives some renewed hope of the possibilities of making radical transformations. New popular instances are, for

example, the young film star Emma Watson as the UN ambassa-
dor for gender equality, with her campaign of 'HE for SHE'. But
sexism, patriarchy and misogyny rule in new forms, as capital finds
ever more ingenious ways of making profit out of gender, sexuality
and sexualization and through GRV.

Inevitably, as social media have expanded, feminist activism may
be both more immediate and less collaborative. These contradictory developments in an increasingly global and marketized world
have implications for how feminist activism is understood, and
has impact on knowledge and understanding. Social media within
neoliberalism have been closely linked to forms of sexualization,
sexting and forms of online abuse, including trolling, in the commercialization of gender and sexualities.

Waves of 'Education Feminism' as Empowering

It is now clear that feminist forms of education, in universities,
in schools and informally, can be incredibly empowering and
creative. As many of the participants in my study claimed, feminist
education and learning had become their life and their passion
across the vicissitudes of changing educational and political contexts (David 2014). This is despite the encroachment of new forms
of managerialism and bureaucracy that embed forms of 'lad' or
'rape culture', sexual harassment, sexism and patriarchal relations
across and within diverse HE. Even though education is not the
only input into women's empowerment, it is nonetheless a central
one, as UNESCO (2012) argued.

We want to go beyond the simple reversal of male domination and power, into female power, to consider how to make
young women, girls and boys feel empowered to contest current
inequities and unfairness in all forms of education and society.
My review of the state of education and what we know about
gender and education, from feminist studies in the first fifteen
years of the twenty-first century, is inevitably cursory, given the
rapid and extensive accumulation of knowledge. It goes beyond

the numbers game, though, as when these ideas were linked with notions of individual choice and individual social mobility, they became incorporated into neoliberal ideologies, policies and politics (Ahmed 1998). Subsequent waves of feminism – especially the 'fourth wave' – have diverged considerably on what constitutes appropriate approaches, education and learning about gender equality and GRV (Henderson 2014; Teekah, Scholtz, Friedman and O'Reilly 2015).

Equity and choice in education became the twin mantras in neoliberal educational politics and policies, into the twenty-first century. These occur where there is the possibility of individual choice and selection. They are now deeply implicated in the organization of schooling across the whole life-course. This search for 'the best' school or childcare, to ensure one's child has the best possible opportunities in terms of later education, employment and career, disfigures and distorts an education that is inclusive, creative and diverse. It puts employment opportunities ahead of well-being and health, not to mention social class, gender and ethnicity, and other forms of equity. It prioritizes economic well-being instead of social and communal well-being. It also ignores the social and mental health costs of such a career.

Metrics belie the structural basis of the education system and links with diversity and inequalities. As education as a whole has expanded, any notion of a coherent 'system' has evaporated. Moreover, it also becomes increasingly complex to consider appropriate strategies for modifications that would make the system more equal and fair. Underlying a more marketized and privately funded set of educational institutions are more opportunities for individual gains and success and, at the same time, for substantial loss and degradation or belittlement. And indeed, alongside or integral to the new forms of education are strategies of governance to quantify and control the ways that these forms are assessed and evaluated. The 'league table approach to life' has brought with it increasing amounts of anxiety and stress, in terms of how to perform as an educator.

Revisiting the GAP Work Project: What Have We Learnt?

As we have seen, our EU project addressed the specific question of how to challenge gender norms and GRV, including sexist and homophobic bullying, harassment and rape, through *education and training* to challenge these issues amongst children and young people. We started from the presumption that the ways in which adults were educated or trained to deal with these questions needed to be addressed as a priority. We aimed to give educational professionals, such as teachers and youth workers, tools to tackle these questions, based largely on our feminist knowledge and insights. We also extended this, given the particular circumstances of the project in the four countries, to community, health and social workers as a way to pilot our techniques and training.

This was a large and complex project, bringing together feminist academics and activists in various community groups, working across education and health questions as appropriate to the local diverse contexts. Although it was large, we only had a short time period in which to work and focus on addressing our specified challenges around GRV and gender equality. We found that the school curriculum in the four countries in which we worked did not adequately address how to show young girls and boys that the gender norms they see around them, especially in new social media, do not have to be the way they are. They could be more fair and equal, helping children to become more rounded adults and human beings.

We have learnt first of all about the differences between at least the four countries of the EU in which we worked, about the differences in terms of intellectual or theoretical approaches to feminism, education and pedagogies, and about gender equalities and GRV. We are now clear that there are substantial differences between training and education. The training we provided was limited to a skills base, based upon specific knowledge and information about gender norms and sexualities, and upon legal approaches to child protection and safeguarding within the current conjunctures. This means that we did not seek to embed a theoretical approach to gender and sexuality within our training, although we, as researchers, shared an understanding of these post-structural feminist approaches in the twenty-first century. We also used these ideas to develop our thinking.

We have also learnt how well embedded within HE, in some places and contexts, some psycho-social approaches to gender and sexualities are. This is particularly true of the Spanish Catalan University, with its support for a feminist post-structural approach within psycho-social studies. This meant that there was an extensive array of feminist community groups, using feminist pedagogies to work with women and children who might be subject to GRV. This was also evident, although to a much lesser extent, in the Italian case. There the local researcher worked closely with two well-established feminist community groups in Turin to develop training for teachers and health workers. In other words, the resurgence of feminist activism through local and community groups around gender and sexualities, including about GRV, has been growing since the late twentieth century in Italy and Spain.

In the UK and Ireland we learnt, by contrast, about the obstacles to the implementation of any educational or training programme concerning gender and sexualities, particularly for pre-service teachers and youth or social workers. While there has also been a resurgence of feminism within HE and national communities, this resurgence has not had the same impact upon university education as appears to be the case, at least at a surface level, within Italy and Spain. Of course, this may have to do with the circumstances of the particular groups and researchers with whom we were working. We have noted, in previous chapters, just how extensive feminist studies within education, the humanities and the social sciences are. So this may just be an artefact of our applied research and training study.

We are keenly aware of the exceptional work in and on VAWG and GRV in universities. We are aware of, for example, the path-breaking feminist work on sexual harassment, 'laddism' and lad cultures in HE, including critiques of curricula offered, amongst both students and academics (Phipps and Smith 2012; Jackson and Sundaram 2015). While these studies open up critiques of the sexist and patriarchal structures of HE, they do not enable teaching about these issues to pre-service or in-service teacher education as a routine.

We learnt too of how non-normative teaching about gender equality and GRV in schools is in the British Isles. We also learnt that the areas of sex or sexualities and relationships education (SRE), and personal, social and health education (PSHE), together with gender norms or normativity, are not commonly taught in either primary or secondary schools, at least in Ireland and the UK, and teaching in this area is only patchy in Italy and Spain. These courses are not necessarily developed by feminist educators but rather by professionals in health and social education, occasionally drawing on the insights of the social sciences. It appears more likely to be taught and talked about in literature and English teaching, and possibly history or civics, than in courses explicitly about sexual relations. Indeed, it was the case that these intimate and delicate issues of personal, social and sexual relations only came to light tangentially in our training courses and with respect to particular professional issues.

Additionally, we learnt about the obstacles to teacher training and education concerning the preparation of professionals regarding gender equality and GRV. This issue of developing critiques of the structures and practices of education and schooling, including addressing questions of gender norms within particular school subjects, is also not commonly used, but there are clearly differences within and between nations and locales. As educational trainers and researchers, we, in the UK, were prevented from developing pilot programmes on gender equalities and GRV as part of SRE or PSHE for pre-service teachers. As a result of this exclusion, we had to change our research design and move to work with training youth and community workers.

By serendipity, the Irish local-action team had decided to develop this as their curriculum offer for pre-service and in-service youth and community workers. We therefore had comparative evidence about feminist and critical training for these professionals and working with local community groups. But in both Ireland

and the UK, we worked with long-standing community and legal feminist-activist groups such as ROW.

From the UK and Irish cases, we argue the importance of embedding work on SRE, PSHE and questions of gender equalities throughout the school curriculum, in teacher training and in other professional training such as youth, community and social work. What also became clear from our studies was the need for more attention to child protection, safety and laws about this. This awareness and commitment to child protection, including the risks and necessary safeguards against those risks, clearly establishes a significant new development in British policy (Alldred and Biglia 2015).

These areas have been linked not only to issues about children, but also questions of equality, through the revised Equalities Act, 2010. This legislation, brought in by an outgoing Labour administration, was also committed to ensuring ways to enforce such commitments, through a series of 'public sector equality duties (PSED)'. While this was a strong potential measure, covering the intersections of diverse equalities – class, race/ethnicity, gender and disabilities – the incoming Coalition government watered it down. It is being further eroded by a thoroughly Conservative administration, not committed to either the public sector or specific issues of equality. Its potential in maintaining levers to ensure equalities has been seriously eroded.

On the other hand, the move towards legislating about gay marriage rather than gay partnerships has been yet another step along the policy road towards embedding a more equal, subtle approach to social and sexual relationships. This legislation has been passed in most countries of the global North, with the UK making it legal in 2013, and Ireland, along with the US, being one of the last in so doing in 2015.

Nevertheless, the overarching learning from our project has concerned the complexities of gender equalities entwined with GRV. This has enhanced our theoretical and practical knowledge about the difficulties and the creative possibilities of embedding social change around gender consciousness (David 2015b and c). It has also contributed to our understandings regarding the extensiveness of 'violence' as being both symbolic and 'real'.

Most important is the acknowledgement that not all responsibility lies with women and feminist researchers to do the work of caring about change. It is necessary to extend responsibilities to men, including men in power. Indeed, a final step is to get men, and men in power in particular, to take responsibility for GRV. How do we ensure that men who have been in violent and abusive relationships learn how to work on and resolve their issues of violence? They also need to acknowledge the negative impact of particular cultural and gender norms in order to commit to change. The experience of Luke Daniels (2012) in working with men on their violence demonstrates the possibilities and potential of this kind of approach.

Gender Equalities and GRV: An Education

More consideration to the social and cultural contexts in which gender equalities are manifest is necessary. We have, in some aspects of our research, given consideration not only to gender equality but also to the malpractices entailed in thinking through notions of gender norms, normativity and stereotypes in the twenty-first century. Precisely how do we acquire our notions of gender and sexuality in relation to others and how do they become embedded in our psyches? How resistant to change are these early ideas and how can we learn to be more respectful and fair and equal in these complex arenas of social and sexual relationships? How do we learn about and understand, as well as confront, issues around sexual abuse and harassment, bullying and even stronger forms of violence within and across people's lives and across continents?

Quite clearly, these changing notions are situated in political contexts of fluctuating forms of state and civil society. Neoliberalism has brought with it new forms of civil society as well as new forms of state governance, and methods of governance. These have implications not only for education, but also for children, young people and adults, including diverse communities.

Moreover, they cross borders and boundaries, and are often heavily contested.

An increase in warfare, combined with the above issues, has led to forms of war in which there has been a rapid rise in genocide and links with the much under-researched issue of femicide. This has had implications for women and children's lives on a huge scale. Even at a less dramatic level, there is increasing evidence of how war breeds violence, especially GRV. This is in terms of rape and the threats of rape and violence, not only to women but also to children.

Addressing the question of children and safeguarding or protecting them from violence remains a very contested issue, despite the ways in which some safeguards have been put in place officially, for example by the UK Children's Commissioners. However, these safeguards only go some way towards handling the wider civil and criminal issues of child sexual abuse. Furthermore, there has been a growth of charities committed to providing facilities for the care of and attention to vulnerable young children, yet some of these organizations have themselves been subject to harassment.

Take the case, in the UK, of the treatment of Camilla Batmanghelidjh, the colourful British businesswoman who founded and became the chief executive of Kids' Company in 1996. This was a charity providing practical, emotional and educational support to vulnerable inner-city children and young people. In 2015, its services linked to 210 schools and reached an estimated 80,000 children, young people and families whose lives had been disrupted by poverty, abuse and trauma. It operated through a network of street-level centres, alternative education centres and therapy houses, and with over forty schools in London and Bristol, as well as a performing arts programme in Liverpool. In August 2015, the whole programme was closed, ostensibly because of financial mismanagement of large sums of public funding. It appears that this pressure, possibly amounting to harassment, was because of her radical views and abilities to work with vulnerable excluded young people.

Global Campaigns for Girls' Education

A report from the EVAW argues that 'Education policies are failing to protect girls from abuse now, and are not working towards the prevention of future abuse' (Townsend 2015). There are a few signs that VAWG is being given some attention in global education, as a result of this emerging evidence. For example, Malala raised this issue through her valiant struggle against the odds both to survive and to have an education. The honour of receiving the Nobel Peace Prize in 2014, and speaking at the UN in July 2013, raised the profile of girls' education in developing countries. And yet for the most part this is still seen as a distant goal and one that does not affect the global North, except in terms of providing support through campaigns such as those of the actress Angelina Jolie combining forces with the UK government, through the then British Conservative Foreign Secretary William Hague, to mount a campaign against VAWG in Africa.

More recently, in spring 2015, Mulberry School, a London-based mixed-race community school led by a feminist headteacher, has taken up the issues, together with first lady of the US Michelle Obama, and with the former trenchant premier of Australia, Julia Gillard. Back in 2012, Gillard had been the victim of an abusive sexist campaign against her as premier. She was the first to assert publicly that this constituted misogyny, in a powerful speech in the Australian Parliament.

This new campaign for international girls' education was launched at Mulberry, orchestrated by the UN-organized campaign for female education (CAMFED). Despite limitations, it is using some of the insights of feminists. Its focus, however, is largely confined to arguing for the ambitions of girls from black and minority ethnic groups (BME) and how to develop them in West Africa, rather than in the global North.

There are some forms of sexual violence such as female genital mutilation (FGM) that are now discussed openly in the global North, in ways previously unheard of. For instance, a very brave schoolgirl, seventeen-year-old Bristol student Fahma Mohamed, started an online campaign to put education at the heart of ways of dealing with FGM in 2014. She turned her campaign into an anti-FGM charity called Integrate Bristol, backed by two British newspapers – the *Guardian* and the *London Evening Standard*. Her campaign was also opposed by right-wing newspapers, including *The Times* and the *Daily Mail*. Sarah Vine, a *Daily Mail* columnist and wife of the then Conservative Secretary of State for Education, Michael Gove, wrote a particularly virulent attack, saying that it was not of concern to most parents and their children, or to schoolgirls here (Vine 2014). However, the campaigners persisted and, after receiving the support of over a quarter of a million signatures, they took the petition to Michael Gove and he agreed to support the call for information to be circulated to all secondary schools. He also visited the City Academy in Bristol to see their work (February 2014).

The UN Secretary General, Ban Ki-moon, also backed the campaign, agreeing to support similar grassroots campaigns led by local media in other nations. 'Whatever the UN can do to help the campaign we will spare no efforts,' he is reported to have said – 'Ban Pledges UN Support for FGM Campaign' – adding 'I will spare nothing, I will mobilize all UN tools and agencies to help promote this campaign . . . This is part of making women's voices heard and giving them the right to protect themselves' (Alexandra Topping, the *Guardian*, 6 March 2014: 13).

For International Women's Day (IWD), the *Guardian* announced 'FGM Top of Women's Day Agenda' (8 March 2014: 33), with letters from senior women about the matter. One mentioned the speech by Lynne Featherstone, then Liberal Democrat MP and UK development minister, at the Women of the World (WOW) Festival: 'Our experience shows that if we are to see an end to mutilation of girls in our lifetime, we must fight FGM and all other aspects of VAWG wherever it takes place and with every tool at our disposal.'

Baroness Onora O'Neill, the chair of the Equalities and Human Rights Commission (EHRC), wrote in the *Guardian* on 8 March that they felt the

> Government's recent commitment to end this abuse [is welcome] but we are concerned that the steps proposed are not sufficient . . . any

strategy should incorporate proper enforcement of existing sanctions against professionals who fail to report children at risk of or victims of FGM. As a national human rights institution, the commission is well placed to be the single body overseeing this . . . FGM can never be excused by reference to cultural practices that are inconsistent with human rights. Social media campaigns can be highly effective, as we have seen with FGM for instance. (2014: 33)

A panel at the Gender and Education Association (GEA) biennial conference (June 2015) brought together debates about girls' education, which included addressing CAMFED's work, the International Women's Initiative (IWI) led by Amaranta Thomson, and the two Muslim girls from the Bristol school that had been the first to raise an educational campaign on FGM. The debate centred on issues about diverse and changing families and communities and the lack of sustained knowledge regarding sexuality, gender and GRV. Discussions by young feminists about what they learn in school are important as they recognize the extent of inequality in their lives from an early age.

Despite their tangential nature to formal schooling, the various campaigns by celebrities and feminists through WOW give impetus to new ways of working. At the same time, the massive changes in contexts, cultures, civil society and the role of the state have led to consideration of how to develop and embed a more nuanced approach and understanding of well-being and mental health or emotional well-being. So how do we go beyond the achievement, attainment and ambition agendas to thinking about emotional and psychic well-being?

Education in Schools:
Girls and Boys Together or Separately?

The British school curriculum, like those of other countries of Europe and elsewhere, still does not commit explicitly to ensuring gender equality and lessons about GRV. At the very least we need compulsory SRE across all levels of school – from early childhood through to the end of secondary schooling. This British campaign remains a distant dream as attempts to ensure that all children and young people receive some SRE, as well as information about what makes healthy bodies and minds, has never been acceptable as mandatory. The House of Lords turned down an amendment to the Families and Care Bill that would have made SRE compulsory (28 January 2014).

A small demonstration took place on IWD 2014 to try to make SRE compulsory under the slogan *Yes matters*: a modest demand for a proper education for men and women alike to live their lives free from violence, intimidation and lack of control over their own lives. One young girl aged ten told Emma Renold and Jessica Ringrose (2015) that 'If I don't go out with him, they say he will beat me up', another, aged twelve, said, 'If we don't kiss they call us a fridge', and a boy aged eleven said, 'They forced me to go out with her.' So educating about sexual consent and respect is vital and really matters.

As Deborah Orr (2014: 27) argued for IWD 2014:

> teaching children what exploitation is, rather than what consent is, may be a more visceral way of getting across the cowardice and self-delusion of rape . . . in some areas the level of sexual violence and the types of violence inflicted are comparable to how sexual violence is used in wartorn territories . . . Abusing someone who is utterly vulnerable does not make you powerful, but these men don't see that – they instead see the vulnerability as a measure of their comparative strength . . . vulnerability is seen as an invitation, a reason, to rape . . . An emphasis on vulnerability places all the emphasis on the perpetrator, on the one who, in the old euphemism, is 'taking advantage'.

Yet, since the introduction of voluntary sex education into British state schools over thirty-five years ago, few efforts have been made to train teachers in how to teach about these vitally important but sensitive issues. Even teacher education fights shy of including these topics in the curriculum of trainee teachers, not seeing it as germane to healthy and appropriate citizenship.

The WOW Festival Conference 2014 issued paper bags with

the slogan: 'What makes a great WOW education for twenty-first century girls?' This campaign joined together with the wider international campaign – 'A Million Women Rising'. Here we joined forces with the anti-FGM and the Malala movement to demand worldwide changes in the educational lives of women. But, in November 2015, the British Conservative Secretary of State for Education, Nicky Morgan, removed discussion of women's rights and feminism from the A-level curriculum in politics, despite a massive online campaign.

Without SRE, and a linked or joint course in citizenship education, or political education, it remains difficult to embed a transformed gender consciousness. However, our various research studies, from the GAP project to other feminist evidence, have shown how difficult it is to transform gender relations in co-educational classrooms. So we would want to argue for single-sex education, at least for lessons in SRE and about GRV. This should also include discussion about how to work towards fair and equal sexual relationships. In particular, there is growing consensus on the need to develop a consciousness around issues of 'sexual consent' and at what age and stage (Kelly 1988, 2014).

This ideally would be embedded across schools and their curricula from early childhood education to the end of compulsory schooling – a K through grade 12 or 13. This would cover relationships not only between boys and girls, but within peer groups, and in developing diverse sexualities, including lesbian, gay, bisexual, transgender, queer, and intersexual (LGBTQi). This would variously address questions of PSHE and SRE, including through sociology, anthropology and psychology. This subject would consider, in other words, questions about how social and sexual relations are seen in cultural and religious communities, through history to the present day.

Rachel Thomson and Janet Holland (2014) have usefully discussed the notion, in relation to women's social and sexual positioning, of 'the male in the head' and extended it to considerations of 'the mother in the head'. Both of these are important for thinking through issues regarding women's leadership. There is a question of how to embed a gender consciousness through and across the whole school curriculum. For the most part, as Jessica Ringrose (2012) and colleagues show, feminism remains hidden or contested within schools, particularly in the UK.

Why an Educational Manifesto?

In view of this, what would a feminist manifesto for education contain? Such a manifesto would be educational in several respects: not only the formal curriculum of schools and other educational institutions, including higher, professional and adult education, but also the ways in which learning occurs. While education may be constituted in formal organizations such as schools, learning may take place in many different and unexpected contexts. It cannot be captured in one locale or institution. Inevitably, forms of institutionalized education may continue to have economic and social effects, especially on inequalities within and between generations.

As we have seen, there are growing inequalities between socio-economic classes despite the growth and expansion of education, especially HE and professional learning. This growing inequality has therefore become heavily contested both globally and locally, as growing numbers of women continue in education but do not necessarily attain or achieve, or even aspire to, the same outcomes in the social world. We clearly need to give greater consideration to how to create a more inclusive approach to education and learning. We also need to be aware of how gender norms are deeply embedded in more complex social structures and relationships, as well as gender and education as a structure. This means making explicit gender consciousness that is both aware and critical of current forms, relations and structures.

There are examples of good practice in developing the materials on which to base such courses and curricula. The English curriculum in schools may well be a good seedbed for the cultivation of alternative approaches. If teachers are 'free to choose' their texts and materials, there is a growing body of excellent novels that address some of these questions. *To Kill A Mockingbird* (1960) by Harper Lee has long been a classic novel depicting social, sexual (including a rape) and racial life in the Deep South of the US for a young girl. The publication of *Go Set A Watchman* (2015), which was arguably a first draft of *To Kill A Mockingbird*, has elicited a host of critical and controversial comments about the extent of change for women and blacks in the US.

Monica Ali's (2005) prize-winning *Brick Lane* addressed questions of being a young woman in a Pakistani community in London. *I am Malala* (Yousafzai and Lamb 2013), about this brave Pakistani girl who survived a shooting and continues campaigning for girls' education, is also important. Some feminist teachers in some places and spaces are able to take up these issues within their classrooms. There is a possibility that this may become easier in the UK with the development of free schools. In the US, the feminist teacher-blogger Ileana Jimenez has been teaching through this kind of approach for a decade now in a range of private schools on the East Coast, largely but not solely in New York.

Nevertheless, there remain problems about how to tackle these subjects without the teacher education necessary to ensure good practices in school. As we have seen, this remains a difficulty. Similarly, there is very little evidence to show that young people are learning about the violent struggles there have been for suffrage. There are some significant instances of model work on women's and girls' history by important second-wave feminist historians. Moreover, developing an awareness of and sensitivity to gender and sexuality issues cannot be confined to explicit courses and curricula. These issues extend beyond specific subjects alone.

The UK's National Union of Teachers' manifesto, *Stand Up for Education* (2014), did not address gender equality or GRV, but the BERA manifesto for a fair and equal education (2015) made recommendations for a range of issues, also drawing on four decades of educational scholarship. These include the following explicit statements about this policy. Their list takes the reader through the issues for policy as they have been addressed historically through educational research. The list is not exhaustive but it does touch the bases that we have considered. They state:

We want policy that . . .

- develops curriculum for children and young people that supports the democratic values of a diverse Britain – e.g. ethnically, *sexually*, religiously, linguistically, culturally diverse and differently abled . . . (p. 7; my emphasis)

- enables professional education for pre-service and in-service teachers that makes them aware of the hidden ways in which inequalities of 'race', ethnicity, *gender*, class and fixed ideas about ability play out in the classroom and affect the outcomes of children's learning (p. 9; my emphasis)

- funds targeted community-based education like language or *sexual health* classes and has funding that reflects the actual challenges for schools of supporting children and young people with complex and diverse learning needs . . . (p. 11; my emphasis)

- enables children and young people to develop respect for themselves and form mutually respectful social, intercultural and *sexual relationships* with others . . . (p. 11; my emphasis)

- promotes active intervention in all forms of discrimination against children and young people, including overt and implicit racism, classism, *sexism,* homophobia and religious intolerance and listens to the voices of all no matter what their background or the language they speak. (p. 13; my emphasis)

Feminist Education and Our Daughters

The feminist writer Melissa Benn (2013) discussed the dilemmas of being a woman in today's increasingly pressurized, pornified or sexualized and hyper-capitalist society. She provided a map of where we, as women, are and what we can do for the future, through inter-generational conversations about how feminists have dealt with the past and how that can frame arguments on how to work for a better future. She reviewed the gains that feminists have made over the last century and set those against the increasing gulf between rich and poor women, and the rise of the austerity culture, mustering an array of evidence about the changing culture, politics and society, to set an agenda for 'our daughters'.

From the perspective of educators and parents, mothers especially, the first part of the book is where she presented what we know today about schooling and HE, linked together with the increasingly important feminist work on sexuality, sexual abuse and the pornification of our culture for young women. She provided an excellent review of studies on what she calls 'uneasy beginnings': how girls are encouraged and enabled to do better than boys at school and university and this is what now happens. And yet, on the other hand, how this poses a huge problem for girls who are also pressured into becoming a particular kind of sexually attractive woman. This leads to what she calls a 'tick-box culture' in which two key and contradictory elements are being good and being thin. She contrasted this evidence with the important work on how the culture of laddism – male, macho, popular and raunchy – is increasingly pervading HE. She questioned what advice mothers can offer their daughters about sex in this kind of culture of objectification and the myth of perfection. She revisited the debates about puberty and adolescence in the context of single-sex versus co-educational schooling and the changing role of fathers in relation to their daughters. Perhaps most importantly, while Melissa discussed anger as important to this feminist political project (in Part 3), she told us she shied away from anger and the book ends as advice rather than campaigning.

In conversation, she told me that her themes – which particularly highlight the rapidly growing inequality between women, the negative impact of a tick-box, A-star, Oxbridge-obsessed educational culture, and a society that risks becoming increasingly about surfaces – need far more discussion. She added that

> Last autumn, doing a series of talks about the book, I was struck by the many young women who spoke of mid-to-late twenties burn-out and disillusionment, as well as the more familiar anxieties about relationships and having children that remain a huge problem for women within current economic structures and arrangements. So not a list of demands nor indeed, despite the cheery claims of the publisher, a

'manifesto' – I am not a one-woman political party, after all! – but an honest attempt to plait personal and political themes. Writing a book should always change one, in some way. For me, it brought home the vital importance of helping our daughters towards personal, intellectual and political authenticity, a quest that will inevitably throw up a lot of uncertainty as well as generate important social change. Each human life is inevitably an emotional as well as a political construct. No thoughtful parent is going to say: 'Get out there and challenge patriarchy. Job done.' (Melissa Benn, 2 March 2014, for the GEA website)

Concluding Thoughts on a Feminist Education Manifesto

I too am not a one-woman political party, but I find the notion of a feminist manifesto helpful. I want to ensure that the demands of the WLM or second-wave feminism remain of strategic importance for dealing with VAWG and GRV. Feminists have achieved a lot, but equal (educational) opportunities (EEO) still do not include dealing with VAWG or GRV. We need to bring these together for a fair, respectful and dignified future. Forms of GRV continue to distort and dominate the political and educational agenda, embedding abuse, harassment and mistreatment in the everyday lives of women, as mothers, children and young people, and LGBTQi. 'Poverty is sexism' is a mantra that is appropriate to the current conjuncture.

This is a brief argument that Cynthia Cockburn and Ann Oakley (2014), two eminent British feminist professors of sociology, make with respect to transforming interventions on VAW by arguing for a new form of masculinity. In response to revelations that the rate of domestic violence had increased dramatically in the UK over the previous year, such that over 10,000 women had been killed or seriously injured by their 'partners', they ask:

> What category of person carries out these vicious attacks? The 'perpetrators' are their 'partners' . . . Lesbian women perhaps? No, actually: men. (There is a hint: the word 'men' slips into the story once; also

one 'husband' features.) [There is] . . . an urgent need for a conscious social policy to reshape masculinity – for men's sake as well as
women's. (2014: 13)

To extend and elaborate is both appropriate and necessary,
given the rise in international campaigns to stem global violence,
VAWG, killing, murder, rape and sexual abuse, including FGM,
as well as the more common everyday violence, sexism and harassment. These campaigns are part of a new global social movement
of feminists and are pinpointed particularly around IWD, with
what may be considered informal educational strategies through
social media and campaigning, but linked to other more formal
educational institutions, including school, college and university.
(These are what have been called public service announcements
(PSA) in the US.)

Nevertheless, at present, there is a constant shying away from
naming and shaming the perpetrators. It is male violence and
misogyny that must be tackled through any programme of change.
We must aim to change 'the rules of the patriarchal and sexist
game', through education primarily, as we have begun to see.
Even the question of paedophilia is the subject of daily debate:
what are appropriate relations between adults and children, and
when does a child become an adult, or a girl become a woman?
These questions are now germane to any proper discussion of SRE
in school. The question therefore of looking at relations between
men and women, girls and boys, and across and between, has
come on to informal educational agendas, but SRE is still rejected
by politicians, although it is vitally important that young girls and
women are taught about these issues and that they are enabled to
distinguish between appropriate and inappropriate sexual advances,
abuses and behaviour. Otherwise, how can girls and women recognize when they might be subject to, or at risk of, violence or
abuse? How can they know, without education and information,
what predatory and violent men may be up to, and how to resist
or at least not consent?

We must stand together for all our sakes: men and women.
What will it take to grasp the nettle of knowledge that education

is vitally important to make all our lives better – happier and free from constraints and from the threats of abuse, intimidation, harassment, and the risks of GRV, including bullying? We need to transform the way misogyny rules to ensure that women and girls are afforded dignity and respect in all aspects of their/our lives. A proper education about respect and dignity in appropriate relationships between men and women must surely be the best place to start.

References

Acker, S. (1999) *The Realities of Teachers' Work: Never a Dull Moment.* London: Cassell and Continuum

Adams, C., Laurikietis, R. and Johnson, A. (1975) *The Gender Trap: Education and Work: A Closer Look at Sex Roles* (vol. 1). London: Quartet Books

Adams, C., Laurikietis, R. and Johnson, A. (1976a) *The Gender Trap: Sex and Marriage: A Closer Look at Sex Roles* (vol. 2). London: Quartet Books

Adams, C., Laurikietis, R. and Johnson, A. (1976b) *The Gender Trap: Messages and Images: A Closer Look at Sex Roles* (vol. 3). London: Quartet Books

Adams, M., Bell, L. A. and Griffen, P. (eds) (2007) *Teaching for Diversity and Social Justice* (2nd edn). New York: Routledge

Adichie, C. N. (2014) *We Should All Be Feminists.* London: Fourth Estate

Ahmed, S. (1998) *Differences that Matter: Feminist Theory and Postmodernism.* Cambridge: Cambridge University Press

Alberdi, I., Escario, P. and Matas, N. (2000) *Las mujeres jóvenes en España, Colección Estudios Sociales 4.* Barcelona: Fundacion La Caixa

Alderson, P. (2000) *Young Children's Rights: Exploring Beliefs, Principles and Practice.* London: Save the Children/Jessica Kingsley

Alderson, P. and Morrow, V. (2011) *The Ethics of Research with Children and Young People: A Practical Handbook.* London: Sage Publications

Ali, M. (2005) *Brick Lane.* Harmondsworth: Penguin

Alldred, P. and Biglia, B. (2015) Gender-related violence and young people: an overview of Italian, Irish, Spanish, UK and EU legislation, *Children & Society.* DOI:10.1111/chso.12141

Alldred, P. and David, M. E. (2007) *Get Real About Sex: The Politics and Practice of Sex Education*. London: McGraw Hill/Open University Press

Alldred, P. and David, M. E. (eds) (2015) *GAP Work Project Report: Training for Youth Practitioners on Tackling Gender-Related Violence*. London: Brunel University; available at: <http://sites.brunel.ac.uk/gap/resources/reports>

Allen, L. (2001) Closing sex education's knowledge/practice gap: reconceptualization of young people's sexual knowledge. *Sex Education* 1/2: 109–22

Althusser, L. (1971) *Lenin and Philosophy and Other Essays*. London: New Left Books

Anthias, F. and Yuval-Davis, N. (1993) *Racialized Boundaries: Race, Nation, Gender, Colour and Class and the Anti-Racist Struggle*. London: Routledge

Appignanesi, L. (2013) How we got the F-word out of the shade, *The Observer New Review*, 17 March, p. 38

Appignanesi, L., Holmes, R. and Orbach, S. (eds) (2013) *Fifty Shades of Feminism*. London: Virago

Arnot, M. and Weiner, G. (eds) (1987) *Gender and the Politics of Schooling*. London: Hutchinson

Arnot, M., David, M. and Weiner, G. (1996) *Educational Reforms and Gender Equality in Schools*. Manchester: Equal Opportunities Commission, Research Discussion Series no. 17

Arnot, M., David, M. E. and Weiner, G. (1999) *Closing the Gender Gap: Postwar Education and Social Change*. Cambridge: Polity

Atkinson, E. et al. (2009) *No Outsiders: Researching Approaches to Sexualities Equality in Primary Schools*, Full Research Report to ESRC End of Award Report RES-062-23-0095. Swindon: ESRC

Bailey, P. (2007) *Censoring Sexuality*. London: Seagull Books

Bank, B. J. (ed.) (2007) *Gender and Education: An Encyclopedia* (vols 1 and 2). Westport, CT: Praeger

Bank, B. J. (ed.) (2011) *Gender in Higher Education*. Baltimore, MD: Johns Hopkins University Press

Banks, O. (1985) *The Biographical Dictionary of British Feminists*. New York: New York University Press

Banks, O. (1986) *Becoming a Feminist: The Social Origins of First Wave Feminism*. Brighton: Wheatsheaf Books

Banyard, K. (2011) *The Equality Illusion: The Truth about Women and Men Today*. London: Faber and Faber

Barker, D. L. and Allen, S. (eds) (1976a) *Sexual Divisions and Society: Process and Change*. London: Tavistock

Barker, D. L. and Allen, S. (eds) (1976b) *Sexual Exploitation in Work and Marriage*. London: Longman

Bates, L. (2014) *Everyday Sexism*. London: Simon and Schuster

de Beauvoir, S. (1953) *The Second Sex*. London: Penguin

Benn, M. (2013) *What Should We Tell Our Daughters? The Pleasures and Pressures of Growing Up Female*. London: John Murray

Benn, M. (2014) Response to review of her 2013 publication *What Should We Tell Our Daughters?* Gender and Education Association website. Available at: <http://www.genderandeducation.com/tag/miriam-david/>

BERA (2015) *Fair and Equal Education: An Evidence-Based Policy Manifesto that Respects Children and Young People*. London: British Educational Research Association. Available at: <www.bera.ac.uk>

Berelowitz, S., Clifton, J., Firmin, C. et al. (2013) '*If Only Someone Had Listened*'. Office of the Children's Commissioner's Inquiry into Child Sexual Exploitation in Gangs and Groups: Final Report. London: Office of the Children's Commissioner

Biglia, B (2007) Desde la investigacion-accion hacia la inbvestigacion activista feminista. In J. R. Martinez (ed.), *Perspectivas y retrospectivas de la psicologia social en los albores del siglo XXI*, pp. 415–22

Biglia, B. and Luna, E. (2012) Reconocer el sexism en espacios participativos. *Revista de investigación en educación* 10/1: 88–99

Biglia, B. and Olivella-Quintana, M. (2014) Evolution and involution in the sexual and reproductive health services in Catalonia (Spain), *Women's Studies International Forum* 47/B: 309–16, 25 March. Available at: <http://dx.doi.org/10.1016/ j.wsif.2014.02.010>

Biglia, B. and San Martín, C. (2007) *Estado de wonderbra. Entretejiendo narraciones feministas sobre las violencias de género*. Bilbao, Spain: Virus

Biglia, B. and Velasco, A. (2012) Reflecting on an academic practice to boost gender awareness in future schoolteachers. *Education, Society and Culture* 35: 105–28

Biglia, B., Olivella-Quintana, M. and Cagliero, S. (eds) (2015) *Gender-*

Related Violence Legislation in Europe. Tarragona, Spain: Universitat Rovira I Virgili

Biglia, B., Olivella-Quintana, M. and Jiménez-Pérez, E. (2014) Legislative frameworks and educational practices on gender-related violence and youth in Catalonia. *La Camera Blu Rivista di studi di genere* 10. Available at: <http://www.camerablu.unina.it/index.php/camera blu/article/view/2567>

Bloch, M., Holmlund, K., Moqvist, I. and Popkewitz, T. S. (eds) (2003) *Governing Children, Families and Education.* London: Palgrave Macmillan

Bondi, L. (2009) Teaching reflexivity: undoing or reinscribing habits of gender. *Journal of Geography in Higher Education* 33/3: 327–37

Bonet, J. (2007) Problematizar las politicas sociales frente a las(s) violencia(s)i de genero. In B. Biglia and C. San Martin (eds), *Estados de wonderbra: entrejiendo narraciones feministas sobre las violencias de genero.* Bilbao, Spain: Virus.

Brady, S. (2005) *Masculinity and Male Homosexuality in Britain 1861–1913.* Basingstoke: Palgrave Macmillan

Brah, A. (1992) The scent of memory: strangers, our own and others. *Feminist Review* 100/1: 6–26

Brah, A. and Phoenix, A. (2004) Ain't I a woman? Revisiting intersectionality. *Journal of International Women's Studies* 5/3: 75–86

Bristol Women's Studies Group (1979) *Half The Sky: An Introduction to Women's Studies.* London: Virago

Burman, E. (1994) *Deconstructing Developmental Psychology.* London: Routledge

Bustello, M. and Lombardo, E. (2012) Understanding and assessing quality in gender violence policies in Italy and Spain: presentation delivered at ECRP joint session workshop on *Thinking Big about 'Gender Equality' Policy in the Comparative Politics of Gender.* Belgium: Antwerp

Butler, J. (1990) *Gender Trouble: Feminism and the Subversion of Identity.* New York: Routledge

Butler, J. (1993) *Bodies that Matter: On the Discursive Limits of 'Sex'.* New York: Routledge

Byrne, E. (1978) *Women and Education.* London: Tavistock

Callender-Smith, R. (2014) Protection of Harassment Act 1997: from anti-stalking crimes to celebrity privacy remedies. *Queen Mary Law Journal* 5: 23–37

Cameron, D. and Scanlon, J. (eds) (2009) *The Trouble and Strife Reader.* London: Bloomsbury Academic

Campbell, B. (2013) *End of Equality: The Only Way is Women's Liberation.* London: Seagull Books

Campbell, B. (2015) After neoliberalism: the need for a gender revolution. In S. Hall, D. Massey and M. Rustin (eds), *After Neoliberalism? The Kilburn Manifesto.* London: Laurence and Wishart, pp. 69–85

Campbell, K. (2002) Power, voice and democratization: feminist pedagogy and assessment in CMC. *Educational Technology and Society* 5/3. Available at: <www.ifets.info/others/journals/5_3/Campbell.html>

Carlassare, L. (2010) Il Custode della Constituzione. *MicroMega* 4: 55–62

Carvajal, M. I. and Vazquez, A. (2009) Cuanto cuenta la juventud en violencia de género? *Revista de estudios de juventud* 86: 217–33

Carvalho, M. E. et al. (2015) Trajectories of Feminist Academics in Higher Education in Brazilian North and Northeast. Paper presented at biennial GEA Conference, University of Roehampton, 24 June

Coate, K. (2011) Writing in the dark: reflections on becoming a feminist. In K. Davis and M. S. Evans (eds), *Transatlantic Conversations: Feminism as Travelling Theory.* Farnham: Ashgate, pp. 79–93

Coate, K., Howson, C. B. K. and de St Croix, T. (2015) *Mid-Career Academic Women: Strategies, Choices and Motivation.* Report to The Leadership Foundation, 1 June

Cockburn, C. and Oakley, A. (2014) Letter published in *Guardian*, 28 February, p. 37

Colás Bravo, P. and Jiménez Cortés, R. (2006) Tipos de conciencia de genero del profesorado en los contextos escolares *Revista de Educación* 340: 415–44

Collini, S. (2010) *That's Offensive! Criticism, Identity, Respect.* London: Seagull Books

Coll-Planas, G. et al. (2011) *Combating Homophobia: Local Policies for Equality on the Grounds of Sexual Orientation and Gender Identity.* A European White Paper. Barcelona, Spain: Ajuntament de Barcelona

COMPASS (2015) *Big Education: Learning for the 21st Century.* London: Compass

Connell, R. (2007) *Southern Theory: The Global Dynamics of Knowledge in Social Science.* London: Allen and Unwin

Conrad, K. (2001) Queer treasons: homosexuality and Irish national identity. *Cultural Studies* 15: 124–37

Cook-Sather, A. (2007) Resisting the impositional potential of student voice work: lessons for liberatory educational research from poststructural feminist critiques of critical pedagogy. *Discourse: Studies in the Cultural Politics of Education* 28/3: 389–403

Coote, A. and Campbell, B. (1982) *Sweet Freedom: The Struggle for Women's Liberation.* London: Picador

COSC (2014) *National Strategy on Domestic, Sexual and Gender-Based Violence 2010–2014.* Dublin: National Office for the Prevention of Domestic, Sexual and Gender-Based Violence

Creazzo, G. (2008) La costruzione sociale della violenza contro le donne in Italia. *Studi sulla questione criminale* 2: 15–42

Crowley, U. and Kitchin, R. (2008) Producing 'decent girls': governmentality and the moral geographies of sexual conduct in Ireland (1922–1937). *Gender, Place and Culture* 15: 355–72

Cullen, F. (2013) From DIY to teen pregnancy: new pathologies, melancholia and feminist practice in contemporary English youth work. *Pedagogy, Culture and Society* 21/1: 23–42

Daniels, L. (2012) *Pulling the Punches: Defeating Domestic Violence.* London: Bogle-L'Ouverture Press

David, M. E. (2002) From Keighley to Keele: reflections on a personal, professional and academic journey. *British Journal of Sociology of Education* 23/2: 249–69

David, M. E. (2003) *Personal and Political: Feminisms, Sociology and Family Lives.* Stoke-on-Trent: Trentham Books

David, M. E. (2013) A 'mother' of feminist sociology of education? In M. B. Weaver-Hightower and C. Skelton (eds), *Leaders in Gender & Education: Intellectual Self-Portraits.* Rotterdam, the Netherlands: Sense Publishers, pp. 43–61

David, M. E. (2014) *Feminism, Gender & Universities: Politics, Passion & Pedagogies.* Farnham: Ashgate

David, M. E. (2015a) (first published 1980) *The State, The Family and Education*. London: Routledge Revivals

David, M. E. (2015b) Feminism, activism and academe: a personal reflection. *Women's History Review*. Available at: <http://www.tandfonline.com/doi/full/10.1080/09612025.2015.1083245>

David, M. E. (2015c) Gender and Education Association: a case study in feminist education. In *Gender and Education*: special issue *Taking Stock. A Framework?* 27/7: 928–46, ed. Alexandra Allan and Penny Tinkler. Available at: <http://www.tandfonline.com/doi/full/10.1080/09540253.2015.1096923>

Davies, B. (1989) *Frogs and Snails and Feminist Tales: Preschool Children and Gender*. London: Routledge

Davis, K. and Evans, M. S. (eds) (2011) *Transatlantic Conversations: Feminism as Travelling Theory*. Farnham: Ashgate

Deem, R. (1978) *Women and Schooling*. London: Routledge

Delamont, S. (2003) *Feminist Sociology*. London: Sage

Dema, S. (2008) Gender and organizations: the (re)production of gender inequalities within Development NGOs. *Women's Studies International Forum* 31: 441–8

DePalma, R. and Atkinson, E. (eds) (2009) *Interrogating Heteronormativity in Primary Schools: The Work of the No Outsiders Project*. Stoke-on-Trent: Trentham Books

Douse, D. (2013) *Domestic Violence: A Select Bibliography – Commons Library Standard Note*. London: House of Commons Library

Dowd, Maureen (2013) Is Facebook's Sheryl Sandberg really the new face of feminism? *Observer*, 17 March. Available at: <http://www.theguardian.com/books/2013/mar/17/facebook-sheryl-sandberg-lean-book>

Downing, L. and Gillett, R. (eds) (2011) *Queer in Europe: Contemporary Case Studies*. Farnham: Ashgate

Dyhouse, C. (1981) *Girls Growing Up in Victorian and Edwardian England*. London: Routledge

El-Bushra, J. and Piza Lopez, E. (1993) Gender-related violence: its scope and relevance. *Focus on Gender* 1/2: 1–9

Epstein, D. and Johnson, R. (1998) *Schooling Sexualities*. Buckingham: Open University Press

Equalities Review Panel (2007) *Fairness and Freedom: The Final Report of the Equalities Review*. London: HMSO

Equality Authority (2012) Annual Report launch (with Annual Report of the Irish Human Rights Commission (IHRC)) at: <www.ihrec. ie/.../ihrc-and-equality-authority-launch-annual-reports>

European Institute for Gender Equality (2013) *What is Gender-Based Violence?* Available at: <http://eige.europa.eu/category/topics/ domestic-violence>

European Union Agency for Fundamental Rights (2014) *Violence against Women: An EU-wide Survey*. Main results report. Available at: <fra. europe.eu/en/publications/2014/violence-against-women-eu-wide-survey-main-results-report>

Figes, E. (1970) *Patriarchal Attitudes: Women in Society*. London: Stein & Day

Firestone, S. (1970) *The Dialectic of Sex: The Case for Feminist Revolution*. New York: Morrow

Foucault, M. (1973) *The Birth of the Clinic*. New York: Pantheon Books

Foucault, M. (1976) *Discipline and Punish: The Birth of the Prison*. London: Pantheon Books

Foucault, M. (1978) *The History of Sexuality*. London: Allen Lane

Fraser, N. (2013) *Fortunes of Feminism: From State-Managed Capitalism to Neoliberal Crisis*. London: Routledge

Freeman, H. (2015) A female president? Nice, but not why I want Hillary Clinton. *Guardian*, 15 April; available at: <http://www.theguard ian.com/commentisfree/2015/apr/15/female-president-hillary-clin ton-science-equality>

Freire, P. (2000) *Pedagogy of the Oppressed* (30th anniversary edn). London: Bloomsbury Academic

Friedan, B. (1963) *The Feminine Mystique*. Harmondsworth: Penguin

Gill, A. and Mason-Bish, H. (2013) Addressing violence against women as a form of hate crime: limitations and possibilities. *Feminist Review* 105: 1–20

Giraldo, E. and Colyar, J. (2012) Dealing with gender in the classroom: a portrayed case study of four teachers. *International Journal of Inclusive Education* 16/1: 25–38

Goñalans-Pons, P. and Ferree, M. (2014) Practicing intersectionality in Spain. *Quaderns de Psicologia* 16/1: 85–95

Grant, J. (2016) In the steps of exceptional women: the story of the Fawcett Society 1866–2016. London: Francis Boutle

Greenan, L. (2005) *Violence Against Women: A Literature Review.* Commissioned by the National Group to Address Violence Against Women. Edinburgh: Scottish Executive

Greer, G. (1970) *The Female Eunuch.* London: Picador

Griffith, A. and Smith, D. E. (2005) *Mothering for Schooling.* New York: Routledge

Hafner-Burton, E. and Pollock, M. (2000) Mainstreaming gender in the European Union. *Journal of European Public Policy*, special issue 7/1: 432–56

Hall, S., Massey, D. and Rustin, M. (eds) (2015) *After Neo-Liberalism: The Kilburn Manifesto.* London: Lawrence and Wishart

Hamner, J. and Saunders, S. (1977) *Well-founded Fear: A Community Study of Violence against Women.* London: Explorations in Feminism

Hamner, J., Maynard, M. and Stanko, B. (2013) *Women, Policing, and Male Violence: International Perspectives.* London: Routledge Revivals

Haraway, D. (1997) *Feminism and Techno-science.* New York: Routledge

Harvey, R. (2014) FGM top of Women's Day agenda. *Guardian*, 8 March, p. 33

Hemmings, C. (2006) The life and times of academic feminism. In K. Davis, M. Evans and J. Lorber (eds), *Handbook of Gender and Women's Studies.* London: Sage, pp. 23–33

Henderson, E. (2015) *Gender Pedagogy: Teaching, Learning and Tracing Gender in Higher Education.* Basingstoke: Palgrave Macmillan

Heron, E. (ed.) (1985) *Truth, Dare or Promise: Girls Growing Up in the 1950s.* London: Virago

Hewitt, N. (2010) (ed.) *No Permanent Waves: Recasting the Histories of US Feminism.* New Brunswick, NJ: Rutgers University Press

Hey, V. (1997) *The Company She Keeps: An Ethnography of Schoolgirl Friendships.* London: Routledge

Holland, J., Ramazanoglu, C., Sharpe, S. and Thomson, R. (2004) *The Male in the Head: Young People, Heterosexuality and Power*, 2nd edn. London: Tufnell Press

hooks, b (2004) *We Real Cool: Black Men and Masculinity.* New York: Routledge

Htun, M. and Weldon, L. (2012) The civic origins of progressive policy change: combating violence against women in global perspective, 1975–2005. *American Political Science Review* 106/3: 548–69

Jackson, C. and Sundaram, V. (2015) '"Lad culture" and higher education: exploring the perspectives of staff working in higher education institutions'. Presentation at GEA tenth biennial conference, University of Roehampton, 25 June

Jackson, S. (1982) *Childhood and Society*, Oxford: Wiley/Blackwell.

James, E. L. (2013) *Fifty Shades of Grey*. London: Arrow Books

James, E. L. (2015) *Grey*. London: Arrow Books

Jiménez, I. (2013) *The Feminist Teacher Blogger*. New York. Available at: <https://feministteacher.com>

Kearns, N., Coen, L. and Canavan, J. (2008) *Domestic Violence in Ireland: An Overview of National Strategic Policy and Relevant International Literature on Prevention and Intervention Initiatives in Service Provision*. Galway, Ireland: National University of Ireland Galway

Kelly, D. (2001) *Pregnant with Meaning: Teen Mothers and the Politics of Inclusive Schooling*. New York: P. Lang

Kelly, L. (1988) *Surviving Sexual Violence (Feminist Perspectives)*. Cambridge: Polity

Kelly, L. (2005) Inside outsiders: mainstreaming gender violence into human rights discourse and practice. *International Feminist Journal of Politics* 7/4: 471–95

Kelly, L. (2014) Harriet Harman should never have been the target of this non-debate. *Guardian*, 28 February. Available at: <http://www.theguardian.com/profile/liz-kelly>

Kerry, J. (2013) Malala's vital lesson for US foreign policy. *Evening Standard*, 8 March, p. 14

Kim, T. and Brooks, R. (2013) *Internationalization, Mobile Academics, and Knowledge Creation in Universities: A Comparative Analysis*. London: SRHE

Land, H. (1976) Women: supporters or supported? In D. L. Barker and S. Allen (eds), *Sexual Divisions and Society: Process and Change*. London: Tavistock, pp. 108–33

Larumbe, M.A. (2004) *Las que dijeron no Palabras y accion del feminism en la transicion*. Zaragoza, Spain: University of Zaragoza

Lee, H. (2010) (first published 1960) *To Kill A Mockingbird*. London: Arrow Books

Lee, H. (2015) *Go Set A Watchman*. London: Heinemann

Lees, S. (1986), *Losing Out: How Girls Become Wives*. London: HarperCollins

Lees, S. (1993), *Sugar and Spice: Sexuality and Adolescent Girls*. Harmondsworth: Penguin

Lerner, G. (1972) *Black Women in White America*. Philadelphia: Temple University Press

Lerner, G. (1976) *The Female Experience*. Philadelphia: Temple University Press

Lerner, G. (1986) *The Creation of Patriarchy*. New York: Oxford University Press

Lerner, G. (1993) *The Creation of Feminist Consciousness*. Philadelphia: Temple University Press

Lerner, G. (2002) *Fireweed: A Political Autobiography*. Philadelphia: Temple University Press

Lombardo, E. and Bustelo, M. (2012) Political approaches to inequalities in Southern Europe: a comparative analysis of Italy, Portugal and Spain. *Social Politics: International Studies in Gender, State and Society* 19/4: 572–95

Lombardo, E. and Maier, P. (2007) European Union gender policy since Beijing: shifting concepts and agendas. In V. Mieke (ed.), *Multiple Meanings of Gender Equality: A Critical Frame Analysis of Gender Policies in Europe*. Budapest: Central University European Press, pp. 51–75

Luttrell, W. (2003) *Pregnant Bodies, Fertile Minds: Gender, Race, and the Schooling of Pregnant Teens*. New York: Routledge

Luxán, Serrano, M. and Biglia, B. (2011) Pedagogía cyberfeminista: entre utopía y realidades. *Teoria de la Educacion: Educación y Cultura en la Sociedad de la Información* 12/2: 149–83

Mackay, F. (2015) *Radical Feminism: Feminist Activism in Movement*. Basingstoke: Palgrave Macmillan

McIntosh, M. (1968) The homosexual role. *Social Problems* 16/2 (autumn): 182–92. Available at: <http://links.jstor.org/sici?sici=0037-7791%28196823%2916%3A2%3C182%3ATHR%3E2.0.CO%3B2-S>

Maher, F. and Tetreault, M. K. (2001) (eds) *The Feminist Classroom:*

Dynamics of Gender, Race, and Privilege. Lanham, MD: Rowman and Littlefield

Maher, F. and Tetreault, M. K. (2007) (eds) *Privilege and Diversity in the American Academy*. New York and London: Routledge

Malos, E. (ed.) (1995) *The Politics of Housework*. London: New Clarion Press

Marsden, L. (2008) Second wave breaks on the shore of U of T. In W. Robbins et al. (eds), *Minds of Our Own: Inventing Feminist Scholarship and Women's Studies in Canada and Québec, 1966–76*. Waterloo, Ontario: Wilfried Laurier University Press, pp. 210–17

Marshall, C. (ed.) (1997a) *Feminist Critical Policy Analysis I*. London: Falmer Press

Marshall, C. (ed.) (1997b) *Feminist Critical Policy Analysis II*. London: Falmer Press

Martin, J. (2008) Beyond suffrage: feminism, education and the politics of class in the inter-war years. *British Journal of Sociology of Education special issue on Olive Banks* 29/4: 411–23

Martin, J. (2013) Gender, education and social change: a study of feminist politics and practice in London 1870–1990. *Gender and Education* 25/1: 56–75

Maxwell, C. and Aggleton, P. (2013) *Privilege, Agency and Affect: Understanding the Production and Effects of Action*. Basingstoke: Palgrave Macmillan

Mayberry, M. (2001) Reproductive and resistant pedagogy. In M. Mayberry, S. Banu and L. Weasal (eds), *Feminist Science Studies: A New Generation*. New York: Routledge, pp. 145–56

Meaney, G. (1991) *Sex and Nation: Women in Irish Culture and Politics*, Dublin: Attic Press

Middleton, S. (1993) *Educating Feminists: Life Histories and Pedagogy*. New York: Teachers College Press

Millett, K. (1970) *Sexual Politics*. New York: Doubleday

Millns, S. and Skeet, C. (2013) Gender equality and legal mobilization in the United Kingdom: using rights for lobbying, litigation, defence and attack. *Canadian Journal of Law and Society* 28/2: 169–88

Mirza, H. S. (1992) *Young, Female and Black*. London: Routledge

Mirza, H. S (1997) (ed.) *Black British Feminism*. London: Routledge

Montoya, C. (2009) International initiative and domestic reforms:

European Union efforts to combat violence against women. *Politics & Gender* 5: 325–48

Mooney, C. (ed.) (2012) *The Chronicle of Higher Education*. The magazine for academe, in a special issue on 'Diversity in Academe: The Gender Issue', special sections, B3, 2 November. Available at: <www.chronicle.com>

Moran, C. (2011) *How To Be a Woman*. London: Ebury

Morley, L. (2011) Misogyny posing as measurement: disrupting the feminization crisis discourse. *Contemporary Social Science* 6/2: 223–37

Morley, L. (2013) The rules of the game: women and the leaderist turn in higher education. *Gender & Education* 25/1: 116–31

Moss, G. (1989) *Un/popular Fictions*. London: Virago

Mullender, A., Hague, G., Imam, I., Kelly, L., Malos, E. and Regan, L. (2002) *Children's Perspectives on Domestic Violence*. London: Sage

Myrdal, A. and Klein, V. (1956) *Women's Two Roles: Home and Work*. London: Routledge

Nash, M. (2013) *Legislacio I perspectives de genere en la construccio de la ciutadania: una comparatova*. Barcelona: University of Barcelona, AG AUR; available at: <http://www.recertat.cat//handle/2072/21159>

National Youth Council of Ireland (2014) *What is Youth Work?* Available at: <www.youth.ie/nyci/what-youth-work>

New, C. and David, M. E. (1985) *For The Children's Sake: Making Child Care More than Women's Business*. Harmondsworth: Penguin

Newcomb, W. S. and Mansfield, K. C. (eds) (2014) *Women Interrupting, Disrupting, and Revolutionizing Educational Policy and Practice*. Charlotte, NC: Information Age Publishing

Ñuñez, M.-G. (1998) Políticas de igualdad entre varones y mujeres en la segunda república española. *Espacio, Tiempo y Forma* 11: 393–445

NUT (2014) *Stand Up for Education*. London: National Union of Teachers

Oakley, A. (1972) *Sex, Gender and Society*. London: Maurice Temple Smith

Oakley, A. (1979) *Becoming A Mother*. Oxford: Martin Robertson

Obama (2014) *Not Alone: The first report of the White House Task Force to protect students from sexual assault, New York Times*, 22 January; available at: <http://www.nytims.com/2014/01/23/us/politics/obama-to-create-task-force-on-campus-sexual-assaults.html>

O'Brien, M. (1981) *The Politics of Reproduction*. London: Routledge and Kegan Paul

Orbach, S. (1978) *Fat is a Feminist Issue*. London: Arrow Books

Orbach, S. and Winterson, J. (2015) Comments on website. Available at: <http://www.psychreg.com/susie-orbach/>

O'Riordan, T. (2011) *Multitext Project in Irish History*. Available at: <http://multitext.ucc.ie/d/Feminism>

Orr, D. (2014) White House task force to protect students from sexual assault. *Guardian*, 8 March, p. 27

Osborne, R. (2006) Entre el rosa y el violeta (Lesbianismo, feminismo y movimiento gay: relato de unos amores difíciles). *Revista de Estudios Feministas Labrys* 10; available at: <http://www.tanianavarroswain. com.br/labrys/labrys10/sumarioespanha.htm>

Pence, E. and Paymar, M. (1993) *Education Groups for Men Who Matter: The Duluth Model*. Amsterdam: Springer

Penny, L. (2014) *Unspeakable Things: Sex, Lies, and Revolution*. London: Bloomsbury

Phipps, A. and Smith, G. (2012) Violence against women students in the UK: time to take action. *Gender and Education* 24/4: 357–73

Phoenix, A. (1991) *Young Mothers?* Cambridge: Polity

Pillow, W. (2004) *Unfit Subjects: Educational Policy and the Teen Mother*. London and New York: Routledge

Pizzey, E. (1973) *Scream Quietly or the Neighbours Will Hear*. Harmondsworth: Penguin

Rebollo-Catalán, M. A. et al. (2011) Diagnóstico de la cultura de género en educación: actitudes del profesorado hacia la igualdad. *Revista de Educación* 355: 521–46

Rehman, Y., Kelly, L. and Siddiqui, H. (2013) *Moving in the Shadows*. Farnham: Ashgate

Renold, E., Ringrose, J. and Egan, R. D. (eds) (2015) *Children, Sexuality, and Sexualization*. Basingstoke: Palgrave Macmillan

Committee on Higher Education (1963) *Higher Education. The Robbins Report*, Cmnd 2154. London: HMSO

Rights of Women (2010) *Measuring Up? UK Compliance with International Commitments on Violence against Women in England and Wales*. London: Rights of Women

Ringrose, J. (2012) *Post-feminist Education? Girls and the Sexual Politics of Schooling.* London: Routledge

Ringrose, J. and Renold, E. (2012) Teen girls, working class femininity and resistance: re-theorizing fantasy and desire in educational contexts of heterosexualized violence. *International Journal of Inclusive Education* 16/4: 461–77

Ringrose, J. and Renold, E. (2014) 'F★★k rape!' Exploring affective intensities in a feminist research assemblage. *Qualitative Inquiry* 20/6: 772–80

Ringrose, J., Gill, R., Livingstone, S. and Harvey, L. (2012) *A Qualitative Study of Children, Young People and Sexting.* London: NSPCC

Robbins, W., Luxton, M., Eichler, M. and Descarries, F. (eds) (2008) *Minds of Our Own: Inventing Feminist Scholarship and Women's Studies in Canada and Québec, 1966–1976.* Waterloo, Ontario: Wilfried Laurier University Press

Rossi-Barilli, G. (1999) *Il movimento gay in Italia.* Milan: Feltrinelli

Rowbotham, S. (1972) *Women, Resistance and Revolution.* Harmondsworth: Penguin

Rowbotham, S. (1973a) *Hidden from History.* London: Pluto Press

Rowbotham, S. (1973b) *Women's Consciousness: Man's World.* Harmondsworth: Penguin

Ryan, M. (2010) Feminism of their own? Irish women's history and contemporary Irish women's writing. *Estudios Irlandes* 5: 92–101

Sandberg, S. (2013) *Lean In: Women, Work and the Will to Lead.* New York: W.H. Allen

Santos, A. C. (2013) *Social Movements and Sexual Citizenship in Southern Europe.* Basingstoke: Palgrave Macmillan

Shain, F. (2011) *The New Folk Devils: Muslim Boys and Education in England.* Stoke-on-Trent: Trentham Books

Silvestrini, M. T. (2007) Emancipazione de esclusione. Diritti e pratiche delle donne a Torino dalla Resistenza alla Guerra fredda. In F. Balsamo, M.T. Silvestrini, and F. Turco. A sessant'anni dal voto. Donne, diritti politici e partecipazione democratica. Turin: SEB27, pp. 21–46

Skelton, C., Francis, B. and Smulyab, L. (eds) (2006) *The Sage Handbook of Gender and Education.* London: Sage

Slaughter, S. and Leslie, L. (1997) *Academic Capitalism: Politics, Policies, and the Entrepreneurial University.* Baltimore, MD: Johns Hopkins University Press

Slaughter, S. and Rhoades, G. (2004) *Academic Capitalism and the New Economy: Markets, State, and Higher Education.* Baltimore, MD: Johns Hopkins University Press

Stambach, A. and David, M. E. (2005) Feminist theory and educational policy: how gender has been 'involved' in family school choice debates. *SIGNS: Journal of Women in Culture and Society* 30/2: 1633–58

Steinem, G. (2015) *My Life on the Road.* New York and London: Oneworld Publications

Stone, L. (ed.) (1994) *The Education Feminism Reader.* London: Routledge

Strid, S., Walby, S. and Armstrong, J. (2013) Intersectionality and multiple inequalities: visibility in British policy on violence against women. *Social Politics* 20/4: 558–81

Szreter, S. (2006) Obituary of Olive Banks. *Guardian*, 12 December, p. 25

Symonides, J. and Volodin, V. (1999) Human Rights of Women – A Collection of International and Regional Normative Instruments. Paris: UNESCO.

Teekah, A., Scholz, E. J., Friedman, M. and O'Reilly, A. (eds) (2015) *This is What a Feminist Slut Looks Like: Perspectives on the Slut Walk Movement.* Bradford, Ontario: Demeter

Thiara, R. K. (2007) Building good practice in responses to Black and minority ethnic women affected by domestic violence: issues from the UK. In *Ten Years of Austrian Anti-Violence Legislation.* Vienna: Federal Chancellery – Federal Minister for Women and Civil Service, pp. 73–6.

Thompson, N. (2011) *Promoting Equality: Working with Diversity and Difference.* Basingstoke: Palgrave Macmillan (3rd edn)

Thomson, R. and Holland, J. (2014) (reprint) 'Thanks for the memory': memory books as a methodological resource in biographical research. In Jason Hughes and John Goodwin (eds), *Documentary & Archival Research*, vol. 3. London: Sage

Tisdell, E. J. (1998) Poststructural feminist pedagogies: the possibilities and limitations of feminist emancipatory adult learning theory and practice. *Adult Education Quarterly* 48/3: 139–56

Topping, Alexandra (2014) Ban pledges UN support for FGM campaign. *Guardian*, 6 March, p. 13; available at: <http://www.theguardian.

com/society/video/2014/mar/07/un-secretary-general-bank-ki-mo
on-campaign-fgm-video>

Townsend, L. F. and Weiner, G. (2011) *Deconstructing and Reconstructing
Lives: Auto/biography in Educational Settings.* London, Ontario:
Althouse Press

Townsend, M. (2015) Male violence to women 'still unchecked'.
Observer, 29 November, p. 9

UK Labour Party (2015) *Labour's Manifesto for Women.* Available
at: <http://www.labour.org.uk/blog/entry/labours-manifesto-for-
women>

UN (1993) A/RES/48/104 Declaration on the Elimination of Violence
against Women; available at: <http://www.un.org/documents/ga/
res/48/a48r104.htm>

UNESCO (1999) *World Social Science Report.* Available at: <http://www.
unesco.org/new/en/social-and-human-sciences/resources/reports/
world-social-science-report/>

UNESCO (2012) *World Atlas of Gender Equality in Education.* Available
at: <www.uis.unesco.org/Education/Pages/unesco-gender-atlas-
2012.aspx>

UNFPA Gender, Human Rights and Culture Branch (2009) *UNFPA
Strategy and Framework for Action to Addressing GBV, 2008–2011.*
New York: UN Population Fund

UNIFEM (2006) Report by Secretary General of the UN on VAW.
Available at: <http://www.unwomen.org/en>

Vara, G. and Carrasco, L. (2003) Gender equality and the EU: an assessment of the current issues. *Eipascope* 1: 22–30

Vine, S. (2014) Female genital mutilation is a horror our children
DON'T need lessons on. *Daily Mail,* 11 February

Walby, S. (2002) Feminism in a global era. *Economy and Society* 31/4:
533–57

Walby, S. (2011) *The Future of Feminism.* Cambridge: Polity

Walkerdine, V. (1990) *Schoolgirl Fictions.* London: Verso

Walkerdine, V. (1997) *Daddy's Girl: Young Girls and Popular Culture.*
Basingstoke: Macmillan

Walkerdine, V. (1998) *Counting Girls Out.* London: Routledge/Falmer

WE (Women's Equality Party) (2015). *Manifesto.* Available at: <http://
www.womensequality.org.uk>

Weaver-Hightower, M. B. and Skelton, C. (eds) (2013) *Leaders in Gender and Education: Intellectual Self-Portraits*. Rotterdam, the Netherlands: Sense Publishers

Weiler, K. (1988) *Women Teaching for Change: Gender, Class and Power*. Westport, CT: Bergin & Garvey

Weiner, G. (2008) Olive Banks and the collective biography of British feminism. *British Journal of Sociology of Education* 29/4: 403–1

Weiner, G. and Arnot, M. (eds) (1987) *Gender Under Scrutiny: New Inquiries in Education*. London: Hutchinson

West, J. (1980) (ed,) *Women, Work and the Labour Market*. London: Routledge

Westmarland, N. (2015) We can't run away from rape. *THE*, 19 November, pp. 34–40

WHO (2002) *World Report on Violence and Health*. Geneva, Switzerland: World Health Organization

Wikipedia (2016a) *Violence against Women*. At: <https://en.wikipedia.org/wiki/Violence_against_women>

Wikipedia (2016b) *Alva Myrdal*. At: <https://en.wikipedia.org/wiki/Alva_Myrdal>

Willetts, D. (2011) *The Pinch: How Baby-Boomers Took Their Children's Future – and Why They Should Give It Back*. London: Atlantic Books (2nd edn)

Willetts, D. (2013) *Robbins Revisited: Bigger and Better Higher Education*. London: Social Market Foundation

Wilson, E. (1977) *Women and the Welfare State*. London: Tavistock

Wilson, E. (1982) *What is To Be Done about Violence Towards Women?* Harmondsworth: Penguin.

Wolf, A. (2013) *The XX Factor: How Working Women are Creating a New Society*. London: Profile Books

Women's Studies Without Walls (WSWW) (2013) *Doing and Teaching Women's Studies Today*. Conference at the Feminist Library, 20–21 January

Yousafzai, M. with Lamb, C. (2013) *I am Malala: The Girl Who Stood Up for Education and Was Shot by the Taliban*. London: Weidenfeld and Nicolson

Index